Walking the Disused Railways
of Sussex and Surrey

David Bathurst

Photographs by David Bathurst

S.B. Publications

By the same author:

The Selsey Tram
Six Of The Best
The Jennings Companion
Financial Penalties
Around Chichester In Old Photographs
Here's A Pretty Mess!
Magisterial Lore
The Beaten Track (republished as The Big Walks Of Great Britain, republished again
as The Big Walks Of The North and The Big Walks Of The South)
Poetic Justice
That's My Girl
Walking The Coastline Of Sussex
Best Sussex Walks
Let's Take It From The Top
Walking The Disused Railways Of Sussex
Once More From The Top
Sussex Top Tens
Walking The Kent Coast From End To End
Walking The South Coast Of England
Walking The Riversides Of Sussex
Anyone For Tenors?
Walking The Triangulation Points Of Sussex
Walking the Disused Railways of Kent

To Lizanne

First published in 2011 by S.B. Publications
14 Bishopstone Road, Seaford, East Sussex.
Tel: 01323 893498 Email: sbpublications@tiscali.co.uk

© David Bathurst (Text) 2010
© David Bathurst (Photographs) 2010

ISBN 978-185770-360-3

Typeset by EH Graphics, East Sussex (01273) 515527. Email: elizhowe@dsl.pipex.com

CONTENTS

Front Cover: A section of the Chichester to Midhurst line, now incorporated into the Centurion Way footpath.

Title Page: The crossing of the river Wey at the far end of the Christ's Hospital to Shalford walk.

Back Cover: The lovely path beside Pagham Harbour on the Selsey Tram walk.

ACKNOWLEDGMENTS

I would like to thank Lindsay Woods of SB Publications for her encouragement and support; Liz Howe for her splendid work in preparing the text for printing; and my wife Susan and daughter Jennifer for their love and forebearance.

ABOUT THE AUTHOR

David Bathurst was born in 1959 and has enjoyed writing and walking throughout his adult life. He has walked all the complete official long-distance footpaths of Great Britain including the South West Coast Path, the Pennine Way and Offa's Dyke Path, and he has also walked the entire south coast of England, his guides to the Sussex and Kent coasts being published by SB Publications in 2002 and 2007 respectively. By profession David is a solicitor and legal adviser to magistrates in Chichester and Worthing. He is married to Susan and has a daughter Jennifer. When not writing or walking he loves vintage sitcom, teashops, and singing. His most notable achievements have been the recital of the four Gospels from memory on a single day in 1998, the recital of the complete works of Gilbert & Sullivan from memory over 4 days in 2007, and the recital of the complete Handel's Messiah from memory in 2009. Among his scariest experiences is appearing as a contestant on The Weakest Link!

INTRODUCTION

Disused railway walking has deservedly become extremely popular in the last twenty years. Not only does it provide stimulating exercise and a chance to enjoy delightful countryside, but it places us in touch with a very important part of our past and gives a fascinating insight into an era when the railway, rather than the car, was the principal means of transport between both rural and urban centres. There has certainly been an increase in media interest in walking disused railways, evidenced in 2009 by the BBC series of programmes on disused railway walks in Britain, which was quickly transferred to DVD.

Sussex once boasted a formidable collection of railway lines. Whilst the main towns and cities of Sussex are still well served by train, a great many of the lines that opened during the railway boom of the late nineteenth century have now closed down, several of these in the Beeching era of the 1960's. It is inevitable that, forty years later, some of the sections of these old lines will have been swallowed up by modern development leaving no evidence whatsoever that trains may have run across the land concerned. Some sections, however, while still theoretically unavailable as rights of way, are still very easy to trace, and the good news is that an increasing number have been converted into cycle paths and pedestrian walkways, providing an invaluable leisure facility. And even on sections of line where the former trackbed itself is impossible to follow, there's still much evidence that trains once ran, in the form of old bridges, tunnels, station platforms and even station buildings. Many of these lines pass through quite beautiful countryside, making the task of tracing and exploring the old lines all the more rewarding and enjoyable.

The position with Surrey is rather different. Surrey, like Sussex, has been blessed since the 19th century with a prodigious number of railway lines, but its proximity to London and the need for commuter transport to the capital meant that its network of railway lines was hardly touched by Beeching. There are therefore comparatively far fewer disused railway walks through Surrey to be described in this book. That said, those that fall to be described are interesting and, like those in Sussex, well worth exploring.

The purpose of this book is to provide a definitive and exhaustive guide to the walker wishing to follow the disused railway lines of Sussex and Surrey, with information as to the length of each walk, availability of public transport and refreshments, and a potted history of each line. I should point out that not every disused railway line that ran in Sussex and Surrey can be included. It needs to be borne in mind that besides the "traditional" passenger lines that have now been shut, there are numerous other defunct lines that could be described as railways. These include lines which carried freight only, the chiefly narrow-gauge lines which were used for industrial purposes, such as to serve a brick works or a quarry, "pleasure" railways through e.g. public parks and museum/zoo grounds, and urban tramways. To attempt to explore all these lines would in most cases be a task that would be very difficult, very unrewarding or in most cases both. My starting point was, accordingly, to restrict the walks to all the lines that were at some stage a part of the established passenger railway network of the present counties of Sussex (that is to say, East Sussex, West Sussex and Brighton & Hove) and Surrey, including lines that crossed borders into other counties, and which are now closed. However, for completeness, I have also included lines which while not falling into this category are included in the relevant editions of what could be regarded as the definitive works on disused railway lines, namely H.P. White's Forgotten Railways series, Leslie Oppitz's guides to the lost railways of Sussex and Surrey, and Jeff Vinter's Railway Walks. I therefore like to feel I could not be accused of omitting any disused railway line of any significance that ran through Sussex or Surrey at some point in time.

My aim is to provide continuous walks, without detours which can prolong a walk and, because of the need to backtrack, detract from the enjoyment and satisfaction of a journey from A to B. Nevertheless, some straight "there and back" detours are included, usually where I feel they add significantly to the experience of exploring a particular old railway and provide some interesting walking which would otherwise have been missed. It is obviously up to you whether you choose to follow them and that may depend on time available, the weather and how tired you are!

In the descriptions, I have done my best to follow, as far as is possible, the actual courses of the old lines. Sussex is blessed in enjoying many stretches of old line which have been turned into public footpaths and cycleways. But there are still very many more stretches which are not generally available to the public, and in order to provide rewarding old railway walking, there does need to be recourse to some sections which are not officially marked on maps as rights of way and where accessing and following them may not always be completely discomfort-free. The fact is, however, **that if you are walking a section of old line which is not a public right of way and which you have not been given permission to walk, you are trespassing.** Routes described in this book have been carefully prepared and researched to ensure that "legitimate" alternatives are used wherever possible and practicable, including occasions when a parallel road or path enables you easily to follow the course of the old line with your eyes. Where no such legitimate alternatives are available, I have used a number of criteria to determine whether it's appropriate to incorporate, into my described routes, walking over private land. In summary, such land is avoided where to access or walk over it is physically impossible, may (by virtue of obstructions or terrain to be crossed) pose a significant danger or unreasonable discomfort to the walker (you should never be expected to surmount a barbed wire fence, for instance), may cause a significant risk of damage to property (including your own) or interference with wildlife, may constitute a criminal offence (e.g. trespassing onto railway or Ministry of Defence property) or may constitute a fundamental breach of landowners' privacy.

Where on any of my described routes there is a section which is not a designated right of way (and in the interests of providing a more rewarding walk, I have incorporated many such sections), the relevant text will make that clear. **The safest course is always to seek permission from the owner before walking over the piece of land in question.** That is a counsel of perfection; in many cases common-sense will tell you that there will be no difficulty, but if in the slightest doubt it is better to make enquiries and secure permission rather than risk the embarrassment of being challenged by irate landowners, especially if you are contravening a "Private" or "Keep Out" sign or are actually having to surmount a man-made obstacle to access the land concerned. Basic trespassing is not a criminal offence but some forms of trespass particularly where damage is caused may well constitute an offence. Do not think you will always get away with taking the risk, as I know from personal experience that you will not. The relevant sections in the book, by the use of the words "please refer to my introductory notes" (or similar), will make it clear when you are being directed across land which you would do well to consider seeking permission to enter. On occasion, I have specifically indicated that permission MUST be sought to walk a particular section, and suggested alternative routes where permission may not be forthcoming. **For the avoidance of doubt, neither my publishers nor myself can accept any responsibility for the consequences of your trespassing onto land that is not designated as a right of way, without having obtained permission in advance.** Moreover, whilst every effort has been made to ensure the information provided is accurate, land use does change frequently and there may be sections of old line which were inaccessible at the time of writing but which you find to be available, while conversely you may find certain previously accessible sections obstructed when you come to walk them. I therefore recommend you equip yourself with a map before setting out, so that if the way as described in my text is impassable, you can plan and execute an alternative route. Sketch maps are provided at the start of each chapter but an Ordnance Survey map of the section you are covering (the Explorer maps are the best), as well as assisting you if you find yourself with unexpected access problems, will add to the enjoyment of your walk as you can identify places of scenic and historic interest in the surrounding area. You may also wish to supplement your map with a GPS navigational device.

The walks vary in length and difficulty. I suggest you read the introductory sections carefully before opting for a particular walk described in the text that follows. Mileage is only one factor to consider; you also need to take conditions and public transport/refreshment availability into account. There are some walks such as Aldrington to Devil's Dyke that are ideal for a pleasant half-day stroll, while others, including the Redgate Mill-Polegate walk, are logistically demanding, involve some tricky route-finding and could prove very tiring for walkers who are insufficiently prepared. The route descriptions should make it clear whether the route you have in mind is suitable for you to bring a dog or young children. By definition most of the walking is on the flat, but quite a bit of scrambling up and down embankments is required, and there are lots of gates and stiles to negotiate. Moreover, in some places the surrounding vegetation and undergrowth can be quite dense, and although the walks described do not take you through impenetrable terrain, you would be well advised to attire yourself in reasonably stout clothing and footwear. Heavy walking boots are not necessary or recommended; comfortable walking shoes or light boots are best, but whatever your choice of footwear remember that in winter or after heavy rain surfaces can be very wet and slippery.

All the normal advice to those undertaking a walk in the countryside applies. Observe the Country Code at all times. Do not forget wet weather gear when rain is forecast.

Drink plenty of water when the weather is likely to be hot, and don't wait till you are thirsty before you do. Take a supply of food with you too, for even when the route descriptions indicate the availability of refreshments en route, you should always have sustenance to hand just in case. And bearing in mind that you'll need to get home again afterwards, always check public transport availability and times very carefully; it may be prudent to take a mobile phone and have the numbers of local taxi firms handy just in case.

Happy walking.
David Bathurst

PUBLIC TRANSPORT AND REFRESHMENTS

Public Transport
A number of bus operators provide services referred to in the text and the relevant operator is indicated by initials in the preamble to each walk. Service information is most conveniently found on the operators' websites which are also given below.

SC - Stagecoach - www.stagecoachbus.com
CL - Countryliner - www.countryliner-coaches.co.uk
MB - Metrobus - www.metrobus.co.uk
CB - Compass Bus - www.compass-travel.co.uk
BH - Brighton & Hove - www.buses.co.uk
ARR - Arriva - www.arrivabus.co.uk
ESCC - East Sussex County Council Rider - www.eastsussex.gov.uk
EPS - Epsom Coaches - www.epsomcoaches.com

Please note that a number of services do not operate on Sundays or Bank Holidays.

All rail services are provided by Southern, South-Eastern or South West Trains and all offer a Sunday and Bank Holiday service although sometimes trains are replaced by buses at weekends. For more information contact National Rail Enquiries on 08457 484950.

Refreshments
The following abbreviations are used in the preamble to each walk:
P = pub or pubs available; S = food shop or shops available; C = café or cafes available.

LOCATION OF WALKS

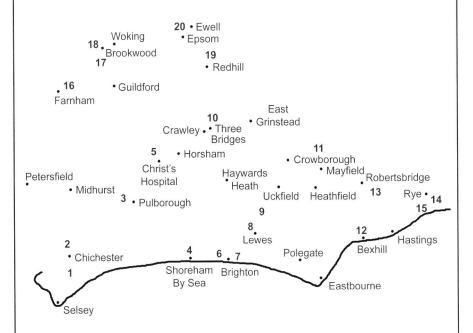

1 Chichester - Selsey	11 Redgate Mill - Polegate
2 Chichester - Midhurst	12 Bexhill - Crowhurst
3 Pulborough - Petersfield	13 Robertsbridge - Bodiam
4 Shoreham - Christ's Hospital	14 Rye - Camber
5 Christ's Hospital - Shalford	15 Rye - Rye Harbour
6 Aldrington - Devil's Dyke	16 Farnham - Ash Green
7 Brighton - Kemp Town	17 Brookwood Necropolis Railway
8 Lewes - Uckfield	18 Brookwood - Blackdown
9 Lewes - East Grinstead	19 Croydon, Merstham and
10 Three Bridges - Groombridge	Godstone Iron Railway
	20 Ewell West - West Park Hospital

WALK 1 - **CHICHESTER TO SELSEY**

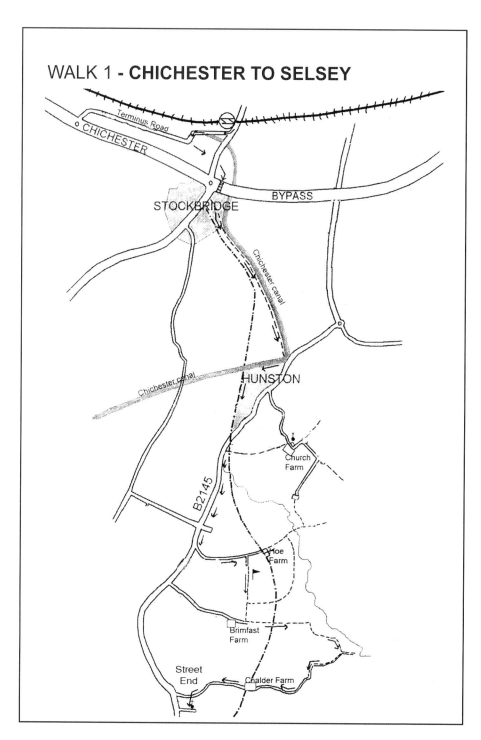

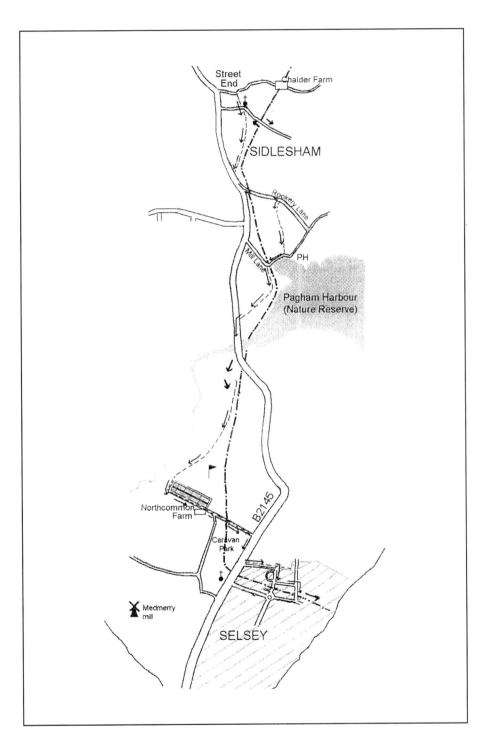

WALK 1 - CHICHESTER TO SELSEY

Length:	9 miles.
Start:	Chichester station.
Finish:	Pond by East Beach Road, Selsey.
Public Transport:	Regular trains serving Chichester on the Portsmouth-Brighton/London Victoria line; regular buses (SC) from Selsey back to Chichester.
Refreshments:	Chichester (P,C,S); Hunston (P,S); Sidlesham (P); Mill Lane (P); Selsey (P,C,S).
Conditions:	This is a very enjoyable and fulfilling walk; while there are many stretches where it is impossible to tell a railway ever existed, and occasions when you are forced some way from the course of the old line, there are some sections of good walking along the course of the old line and sufficient public footpaths linking them up to ensure road walking is kept to a minimum. The walking is across the flat Manhood Peninsula, with lovely views back to the Downs and across Pagham Harbour. You will need at least half a day to complete the walk.

History

The Selsey Tramway was one of the most remarkable railway lines in England, consisting of a stretch of line just eight miles long boasting no less than eleven stations. It was constructed in response to a perceived demand for a rail link between the bustling cathedral city of Chichester and the seaside village of Selsey, with the potential for this small fishing community to become a popular resort. The railway had arrived in Chichester in 1846, but it was not for another fifty years that a company, known as the Hundred of Manhood and Selsey Tramway Company, was formed and duly built the line from Chichester to Selsey. It was officially designated as a tramway rather than a railway to enable the company to escape the rigorous safety measures required for it to become a Light Railway. The engineer was one Holman Stephens, universally acclaimed as a champion of the small railway, being involved in the construction and management of at least 15 different railways. They were characterised by primitive rolling stock, dilapidated buildings and minimal facilities, but boasted a bucolic charm and individuality that other railway operations lacked. The Selsey Tramway, which opened on 27th August 1897, was typical of Stephens' work. It was constructed on a shoestring, with very basic station architecture, extraordinarily old rolling stock - one locomotive was 58 years old when it arrived on the Selsey Tramway - and no crossing gates or signalling, which led to a series of road accidents. In later years, Stephens introduced railbuses onto the line, which although economical gave passengers a particularly uncomfortable ride. The number of stations was amazing, considering how few settlements of any size existed between the two termini. The first stop out of Chichester was at the village of Hunston; then came the three halts of Hoe Farm, Chalder and Mill Pond, before the village stop at Sidlesham. Beyond Sidlesham was the tiny Ferry station, followed by Golf Club Halt, and then three stations in Selsey itself, namely Selsey Bridge, Selsey Town and Selsey Beach. The stretch of line between Town and Beach did not open until nearly a year after the rest of the line, and was to close shortly before the First World War. Even the "village" stations, Hunston and Sidlesham, boasted no more than corrugated iron sheds, while Golf Links Halt offered no more than a platform. The journey time varied; in summer 1913 one train was timetabled to complete the journey in 25 minutes whilst a 1934 timetable shows a journey time of 45 minutes.

By the time war broke out in August 1914, more than 80,000 passengers were using the line each year, for both work and leisure-related activity, and this figure rose to over 100,000 during the penultimate year of the war. The line also carried a tremendous variety of freight, ranging from milk and sugar to bricks and stone; two particularly colourful users of the line were Emidio Guarnacchio who transported ice cream to sell to holidaymakers in Selsey from his store in Chichester, and Colin Pullinger who had

The remains of the Selsey Tram crossing of the canal at Hunston.

a flourishing mousetrap business in Selsey and used the Tramway to transport mousetraps away from the village. One delightful aspect of the operation of the Selsey Tramway was the very personal service which passengers received. Train staff seemed quite happy to wait for tardy passengers and in some cases even walk to the home of intending travellers to advise them that the train was waiting for them. The train staff themselves would often stop the trains to enquire of nearby farmers if they would have produce for transport the next day, or to gather lineside greenery. Not surprisingly, the line developed a reputation for delays, caused not only by the antics of the staff but also by straying animals and accidents arising out of the lack of

Two views of the lovely path beside Pagham Harbour on the Selsey Tram walk.

crossing gates. One particularly memorable incident was on August Bank Holiday 1908 when a train packed with holidaymakers returning from Selsey to Chichester had to be held at Sidlesham when it was discovered the guard had omitted to get on, and the engine had to be sent back to Selsey for him.

The line suffered a setback in December 1910 when a heavy storm resulted in the breaching of the shingle bank separating the sea from reclaimed agricultural land at Pagham Harbour, and submerged the Tramway between Sidlesham and Ferry. Thankfully funds were available to effect the necessary repairs and the line reopened six months later. Disaster then struck in September 1923 when a northbound train was derailed just beyond Golf Links Halt, and one of the crew was killed. With many passengers already deserting the Tramway for road transport, the accident, which was at least partially attributable to neglect in the upkeep of the line, could not have come at a worse time. The 1920's and early 1930's saw a steady decline in the number of trains and passengers. Whereas a dozen trains each way had run on weekdays in 1913, that number was to have halved by 1933; as for passengers, it is recorded that the 11.40am train from Chichester to Selsey on a Saturday in August 1933 carried no passengers at all, and a typical day in 1934 might see just eighteen passengers board the train at Selsey for the journey to Chichester. Meanwhile, the railway company plunged deeper into debt, and with the Southern Railway unwilling to purchase the line, it was only a matter of time before the line closed for good, and indeed the last train on the Selsey Tramway ran on 19th January 1935. The line was gradually dismantled and the buildings demolished; the absence of conventional signalling and other railway landmarks such as bridges meant that evidence of the line's existence was virtually extinguished. It does however live on in the memory as a line of special and unique character, and, as one commentator put it, "It created few artefacts but it left a legacy of admiration and nostalgic smiles".

Walking the Line

Starting from the main forecourt of Chichester railway station, turn right and cross over the railway, following Stockbridge Road, almost immediately passing the John Wiley buildings which are to the right. Just past the Wiley complex on the right there's a gate with a combination entry next to it; if it's closed, follow the instructions at * below, but assuming it's open, pass through it and go straight on along the path, going forward to a road. You're now following more or less exactly the course of the old line, the Wiley complex built on what was the start of the Tramway. The road veers left to arrive at a junction with Terminus Road (*if the path just past Wiley's is inaccessible, you'll need to walk on to Terminus Road, turn right and follow it to the same point). Now enter the huge Chichester Gate leisure complex immediately south of Terminus Road at this point, and accessible from the junction; by following it past McDonald's to the Kentucky Fried Chicken (KFC) restaurant you are continuing to follow the course of the old line, but immediately beyond KFC is the A27 Chichester bypass, which is inaccessible.

Accordingly, you'll need to turn back and cross the complex diagonally to the top right-hand corner and exit the complex, going on into Stockbridge Road. Turn right into Stockbridge Road, follow the road to the A27 roundabout and go straight over, using the footbridge provided, to follow this road (the A286 Witterings road) briefly. Shortly there's a cycle shop on the right-hand side, and opposite this is a concrete footpath (1) going off to the left. If you wanted to follow a little more of the course of the old line you could walk a bit further alongside the A286, turn right into Stockbridge Gardens, right again into Wiston Avenue and on into a children's play area; the old line followed a course through the play area then curved south-eastwards into an area that is now completely swamped with new houses. It's impossible to follow the course of the old line through the housing, so backtrack to the path at (1) above, and follow it. The footpath takes you through a modern housing development, then having crossed a road brings you to the west bank of the Chichester Canal, being reasonably faithful to the course of the old line throughout. Now following immediately to the left of the course of the old line, which was up on a low embankment to the right, you enjoy a delightful canalside walk. After a few hundred yards the old line struck out slightly west of south; it is not possible to follow beside it, but you can follow the course of it from a distance as you continue along the canal bank to Hunston. Just at the end you cross the canal, enjoying beautiful views back to Chichester, and arrive at the road at the northern end of Hunston. Turn right to follow the road briefly, then cross the canal again and shortly turn right again along the left bank of the canal as it heads south-westwards. In a quarter of a mile or so you arrive at what remains of the old drawbridge used to convey the Tramway over the canal. Turn left onto a public footpath which follows the course of the old line past housing on the edge of Hunston, including a road named Tramway Close, and in due course you arrive at the B2145 Chichester-Selsey road.

So far you have been able to follow the old line for most of its course from Chichester, but for the next couple of miles you will be unable to follow any of it, the course of the old line being across private farmland and then a golf course with no means of access. Cross the B2145 and turn right to follow along its left-hand side, taking great care as the road is very busy and there's no pavement. The old line followed parallel with the road initially, then struck out south-eastwards across the fields heading for what is now a golf complex; there's no point in trying to cut across the fields as your progress is blocked by ditches, so you need to continue past Kipson Bank and then turn left along the golf complex approach road. You can see the clubhouse ahead, built on the site of Hoe Farm station on the tramway. However, don't go all the way to the clubhouse, but a couple of hundred yards short of it turn right onto a clear and very obvious signed path which heads southwards towards Brimfast Farm. You pass more golf holes and cross a plank bridge over a narrow stream, going forward to reach a T-junction with another path just by the farm buildings. Turn left to join this path; almost immediately you'll arrive at the point where the old line crossed, and you can trace its course from the clubhouse which you may just be able to make out to your left. However you can't join the old line between Brimfast and Chalder, and you'll need to to make the link by means of a delightful footpath through the fields just to the east.

Follow the footpath heading just south of east beyond Brimfast; its course is obvious, proceeding to the right bank of the Bremere Rife. Follow the bank, swinging sharply left with the rife, then as the rife itself veers off left (north-eastwards) you bear right with the path and go forward to arrive at a farm track. Turn right now onto the track which twists and turns, heading in a generally south-westerly direction, then veers just north of west and proceeds through the Chalder Farm complex. Beyond the complex, follow the track just west of north, and if you look carefully, you can see what remains of Chalder station platform on a field edge to your left. Again, there is no other trace of the old line coming down from Brimfast and heading on towards Sidlesham. Just adjacent to the old platform is a

For tightrope walkers only - the Selsey Tram at the bottom end of Pagham Harbour.

sign warning you to keep out of the adjacent field in order to preserve the delicate wildlife in this delightful area; accordingly, continue on along the farm track past Holborow Lodge, a cat and rabbit rescue centre, to enter the village of Sidlesham. As the track widens and bends sharply to the right, bear left through the main gates leading to the parish church, and follow the church path. Instead of going up to the church door, however, bear left along a path that runs past the left-hand side of the church, exit the churchyard and walk down to a metalled track; turn left onto this track, and walk along it as far as the Marsh Farm sign where another track goes off to the left (2). You can now look back to the edge of the field adjacent to which the old Chalder platform is sited, and follow the course of the old line with your eyes as it heads south-west along this field edge. Now walk back a short distance from the track junction at (2) above, pass the boundary hedge and turn left along the edge of a very large field, the course of the old line passing roughly down the middle of it. Pass to just the other side of the ditch coming in from the right, then bear right to follow the bank of the ditch to the far right-hand edge of the big field, picking up a public footpath here. Now bear left to follow this footpath which brings you back to the B2145, and on reaching this busy road turn left to walk beside it as far as the turning to Rookery Lane. Fortunately a pavement is provided. On this short stretch of roadside walking, look out on your left for Mill Pond Cottage, reminding you that very close by was Mill Pond Halt, one of the stations on the old line but without sidings or station buildings.

Turn left into Rookery Lane, almost immediately crossing the course of the old line, and proceed along it in a south-easterly direction. Very soon the road bends subtly to the left, heading roughly eastwards, but if you look in a south-easterly direction from the bend, across an area of uncultivated rough grass, you can see the course that the old line took. However it can't be followed on to Pagham Harbour, so stay on the road then in a few hundred yards turn right onto a signed public footpath and follow this path; it

soon bends to the left and proceeds pleasantly in the shade of trees down to Mill Lane, the course of the tramway running virtually parallel with it to your right. At Mill Lane, you reach the edge of the quite beautiful Pagham Harbour. By detouring left here you will soon reach the inviting and popular Crab and Lobster pub, but your way is to the right along the road, shortly reaching a signed path going off to the left, along the course of the old line. Before turning left onto the path, look to the right to observe the course of the old line heading north-westwards back towards Mill Pond Halt.

There now follows what is unquestionably the highlight of the walk, with a quite delightful promenade along the shores of Pagham Harbour, following the course of the old line. It was this section that was submerged in 1910, and today it forms part of the Pagham Harbour Nature Reserve, so you are likely to share this part of the

A rare walkable section of the Selsey Tram between Ferry and Selsey.

walk with birdwatchers as well as daytrippers. Sidlesham station building was situated immediately beyond Mill Lane; in the early days of the running of the old line, the name was spelt Siddlesham on the signboard, reflecting its pronunciation. Following the 1910 floods the station building was lifted and replaced at right angles to the track, so that it had its back to the prevailing winds. You proceed through the nature reserve, sticking to the course of the old line heading firstly just east of south and then swinging just west of south. In due course you approach a rife, that is a channel of water which is effectively an inlet of Pagham Harbour, and as you do so, you can clearly see the remains of the old railway bridge crossing straight ahead. If you are a seasoned tightrope walker you could try making your way across it, but realistically you will need to swing right to follow the path away from the course of the old line, parallel with the water channel and almost up to the B2145 where a T-junction of paths is reached. Turn left at the T-junction and proceed round the edge of the water, reaching another T-junction of paths on the other side; you need to turn right here to continue towards Selsey, but if you want to walk a little more of the Selsey Tramway you can detour left here and follow a good path along the south side of the water, soon drawing level with the old bridge crossing. At this point, you can look and walk to your left, following the line back to the water, and/or look to your right into the back garden of the house "Wayside" to see how the line continued. Then retrace your steps, going forward to the B2145.

Cross the road with care, turn left round a sharp bend, then almost immediately after rounding the bend, turn right along a signed footpath towards the buildings of Ferry Farm. This runs parallel with, and just to the right of, the course of the old line. As you reach the farm buildings, bear right onto a signed footpath that goes round the side of the buildings, then swings left to arrive at a wide track which is on the course of the old line (you can look back from here at the course the old line followed from the farm buildings, but can't access it). Bear right now to follow the old line briefly, but your walk along the old line is sadly short-lived; soon you arrive at the northern end of Selsey golf course, and a public footpath sign which draws you away from the old line. The old line continued along the east fringe of the golf course but strict warning signs make it clear that it cannot be followed, so you must proceed along a rather muddy path along the west side of the golf course, gradually getting further away from the old line! Beyond the golf course is a caravan park, and it is here that you need to look out for a signed footpath pointing to the left; take this footpath which heads south-eastwards, initially past rows of caravans and then the buildings of Northcommon Farm. Shortly beyond the farm a tarmac drive leads off to the left, up to the golf clubhouse, and looking just to the right of this drive you can identify the route of the old line by the course of the electricity wires along the right-hand side of the golf course. Golf Links Halt used to stand just a little beyond where the clubhouse is sited today.

You continue south-eastwards along the public footpath, effectively a driveway and the main access road to the golf club from the main road; the course of the tramway is over a field to your right and then through a caravan park, but it is inaccessible for walkers.

Shortly you reach the main road and turn right to follow the main road south-westwards until you reach house no.30 on your right, just beyond which you can look down at an embankment at the foot of which is a small pond. This is the site of Selsey Bridge station and the point at which the old line went under the main road. On the opposite side of the road is a signed footpath leading away to the east; follow this path, while looking to your right at the course of the old line, set in a cutting that is now quite thick with vegetation. This is the last evidence of the old line that you will see. Keeping to the path, you continue round the right-hand edge of a new housing development, and soon reach the north fringe of a red-brick housing estate with easy access to that estate. Now turn right to follow the road heading southwards through the estate, shortly passing the crescent-shaped Denshare Road which lies to your right. Just beyond Denshare Road, Mountwood Road goes off to your left, and the point where it does so is very roughly the site of Selsey Town station; follow Mountwood Road, now very close to the course of the old line on its final leg towards Selsey Beach. You arrive at T-junction with Manor Lane, turning right to follow it to a junction with Beach Road, and here you turn left, passing a parade of shops and bus stop, and go forward to a road junction immediately beyond which is a pond. Turn left just before the pond and follow it round, with East Beach Road immediately to your left. Very soon you arrive at an open area and car park, which stands on the site of Selsey Beach station; the course of the old line is lost in the housing on the land side of East Beach Road. You may be unable to resist the temptation to climb up onto the bank adjoining the shore, perhaps thinking back to the holidaymakers who would have jumped off the train all those years ago and done just the same! Your walk is over and it just remains for you to retrace your steps briefly to the parade of shops, which at the time of writing included a little café as well as a newsagent and foodstore; more potently, perhaps, there's a bus stop just over the road from the shops from where you can catch a bus back to Chichester.

An enterprising initiative saw parts of the walk along the old lines to Selsey waymarked. Sadly the "Selsey Tram Way" can't be found on any Ordnance Survey maps!

WALK 2 - CHICHESTER TO MIDHURST

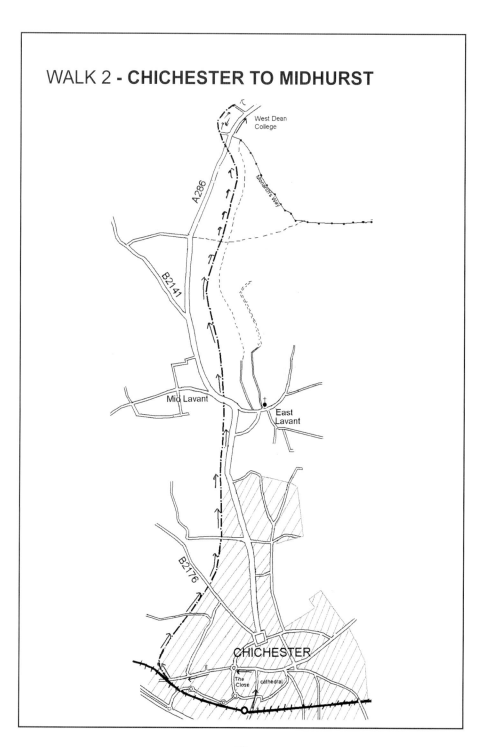

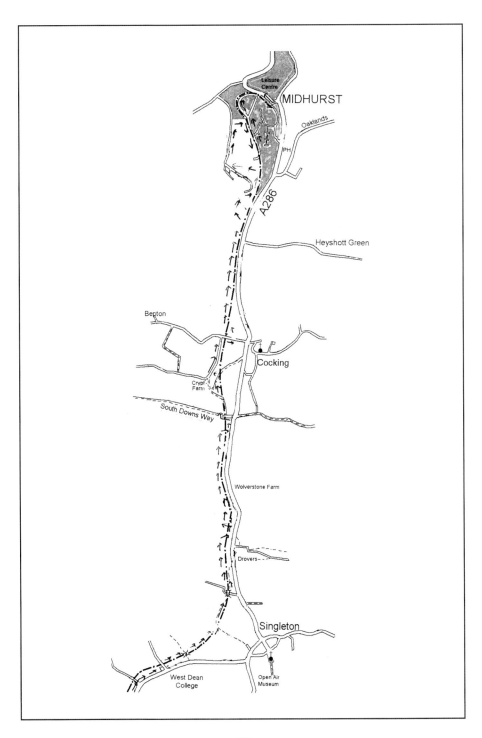

MIDHURST

Leisure Centre

Oaklands

IPH

A286

Heyshott Green

Bepton

Cocking

Crypt
Farm

South Downs Way

Wolverstone Farm

Drovers

Singleton

West Dean
College

Open Air
Museum

WALK 2 - CHICHESTER TO MIDHURST

Length:	12 miles.
Start:	The Cross, Chichester.
Finish:	Bourne Way, Midhurst.
Public Transport:	Regular trains serving Chichester on the London Victoria/Brighton and Southampton/Portsmouth line; regular buses (SC) from Midhurst back to Chichester.
Refreshments:	Chichester (P,C,S); Lavant (P); West Dean (P); Singleton (P,C,S); Cocking (P,C,S); Midhurst (P,C,S).
Conditions:	The first part of the route, as far as Binderton, provides excellent walking along the old line, and while beyond Binderton the old line is not followed by designated rights of way at any stage, it is walkable for much of its course. The result is a really splendid and rewarding walk through quite delightful countryside. You should allow a full day to walk it and enjoy the many interesting features as well as amenities that lie close to or on the route.

History

The idea for a line between Chichester and Midhurst emerged in the 1860's, during a time of intense railway-building activity. The prospectus stated that among the aims of the line was to allow Chichester and Midhurst to sustain their important agricultural and mercantile connection, but also at the forefront of the minds of the Chichester to Midhurst Railway Company must have been the appeal of a direct route from the busy town of Midhurst towards Goodwood and its racecourse, the historic cathedral city of Chichester, and of course the sea. Authorisation was given to construct the rail link in 1864 and work commenced in 1865, only for the project to be abandoned in 1865 because of lack of funds. The scheme was revived in 1876 by the London, Brighton & South Coast Railway (LBSCR), who had initially been less than enthusiastic, and the line linking Chichester and Midhurst finally opened on 11th July 1881, the West Sussex Gazette pointing out that what had been a three hour journey by train to Midhurst from Chichester, via Pulborough or Petersfield, could now be accomplished in forty minutes. The first train of the day left Midhurst at 7am, reaching Cocking at 7.10am, Singleton at 7.21am, Lavant at 7.30am and Chichester at 7.41am. No expense was spared by the LBSCR in the construction of the line, with all three intermediate stations, at Lavant,

Singleton and Cocking, boasting impressive mock timber-framed buildings with moulded stucco panels. Singleton station was built to cater for Goodwood race traffic, with two island platforms and extensive sidings, and indeed the summer months saw thousands of race-goers alighting at this station; at the end of the 19th century the Prince of Wales used the station when visiting West Dean Park nearby. One curious feature of Singleton station was that it boasted one of the largest gentlemen's toilet blocks ever built for a country station! And Cocking station building, the final stop on the journey northwards from Chichester, was another impressive structure, with extravagant ornamentation and floral patterns in the plasterwork. The line involved a climb towards a gap in the South Downs and subsequent descent to Midhurst, and three tunnels were needed, at West Dean (443 yds), Singleton (744 yards) and Cocking (740 yards); one former passenger recalls his anxiety as the train gathered speed downhill through Cocking tunnel, accompanied by a whistling sound that affected his ears! With the lavish station buildings and the three tunnels, it is not surprising that the cost of the line was considerably higher than average, working out at £25,000 per mile.

An 1890 timetable shows six passenger trains every weekday and Saturday in both directions, but no passenger services on Sunday, although for just a few years prior to World War 1 there were three Sunday journeys, and there was an extra Wednesday train for the Chichester market. After World War 1 the six daily trains were reduced to five. Most of the trains in fact ran to and from Pulborough, and for a time in the 1920's there was a train leaving Chichester at 8.15am on the Midhurst line that ran all the way to London Victoria. The line never attracted the number of passengers expected of it, and as early as World War I passenger traffic was declining; buses proved more convenient, comfortable and economical, and although for a while the railway company tempted some passengers back with the introduction of a railmotor train, they still could not provide cheaper fares than the bus company. After World War 1, many people started coming to Goodwood races by car, and during the 1920's and 1930's more and more traffic, both passenger and freight, was lost to the roads. Passenger services were withdrawn on 6th July 1935, although freight services continued. The line came into its own in somewhat unusual circumstances during World War 2, when the Singleton and Cocking tunnels on the line were both used for the storage of wagons containing shells, landmines, torpedoes and other naval ammunition, all of which had to be shunted out as and when required - a particularly laborious task. The Germans attempted to bomb the tunnels on one occasion but the bombs fell on West Dean tunnel where no ammunition was stored!

The most destructive incident in the line's history, however, which could be said to have sealed its doom, was the collapse of a bridge north of Cocking on 19th November 1951, the bridge having been undermined by heavy rain; the line was thus left without a supporting bank at a time when a goods train was approaching, and had the crew not fortunately seen the danger in time and been able to jump clear, they would certainly have been killed. The engine carried on until the track collapsed under its weight, but although it took several weeks to free it, it was later able to be restored to service. As a result of the accident, through services between Midhurst and Chichester were forced to cease at once, and freight services ceased at Cocking and Singleton on 28th August 1953, less than two years after the bridge collapse. Lavant, however, was in that year to become the railhead and loading point for sugar beet from a wide area; it remained in use for freight until 3rd August 1968 and for sugar beet until January 1970. Curiously, the line from Chichester to a point just south of Lavant was reopened in 1972 for the transport of gravel from Lavant to Drayton just east of Chichester, but this usage ceased in 1991 and the track was duly pulled up in 1993. A railway preservation society was formed in the hope of reviving services as far as Singleton, but to no avail, and as will be seen below, much of the southern section of the line has been converted into a cycle track and pedestrian walkway.

A profusion of spring vegetation at the southern end of the Chichester-Midhurst walk.

Walking the Line

Beginning from the Cross in the centre of Chichester, follow West Street past the cathedral to a roundabout; go straight over the roundabout into Westgate, and follow Westgate away from the city centre, arriving at a mini-roundabout with Sherborne Road leading off to the right. Cross over the mini-roundabout and continue along what is a cul-de-sac for vehicles, towards a pedestrian crossing over the main Chichester-Portsmouth railway line. If you continue to the crossing, known as the Fishbourne Crossing, and look down the railway to your right, it's just a short distance from where you are standing to the point where the Chichester-Midhurst railway branched off to the right. However, before you reach the crossing, you will see a bus turning area on the right-hand side. From the bus turning area a concrete path leads off to the right, and you follow this path, keeping the buildings and grounds of Bishop Luffa School to

26

your right, very soon joining the course of the old line. Take a look back along its course to the junction with the main line, then proceed up the concrete path.

This first section of the old line has been converted into a first-class footpath/cycle track known as the Centurion Way, and has become immensely and justifiably popular with walkers and cyclists. Save for one or two fairly short deviations, you'll be able to follow the course of the old line all the way to Binderton, beyond Lavant, using the Centurion Way. Until the first overbridge, carrying the B2178 Chichester-Funtington road, there is really lovely open countryside to the left and, beyond the Bishop Luffa school buildings, suburban housing to the right. Beyond the B2178 overbridge, the line begins to take on a more rural feel; cuttings that are thick with vegetation line each side of the path and although there is housing occasionally visible to the right, you feel as though you are moving out of suburbia. There follow two overbridges in close succession, the second conveying the picturesquely-named Brandy Hole Lane, and if you fancy a scenic detour, there is a signpost to Brandy Hole Copse just before this bridge. Beyond the Brandy Hole Lane bridge, you pass further modern housing to the right, followed by a tall embankment, and for a while the path actually runs slightly to the left of the course of the old railway. To your left, beyond a more modest cutting, is a sizeable area of rolling grassland, and you can look beyond this grassland to the attractive hills of Kingley Vale Nature Reserve. Your path now rises quite abruptly, and as you ascend to meet the top of the embankment you are reunited with the course of the old line. Note the extraordinary modern sculpture by David Kemp right beside the path close to this point, named The Chichester Road Gang, and one of a number of pieces of sculpture work close to or on the Centurion Way. Very soon you pass under the bridge carrying the road known as Hunters Race; just before the bridge there is a slipway giving access to Hunters Race, and a little way down the road to the left is a small car parking area. A signpost by the slipway indicates that Lavant is half a mile away along the Centurion Way, and there is an arm of a signpost pointing up the slipway for Goodwood, West Stoke and East Ashling. Beyond the bridge, the countryside is still open to your left but the houses of Lavant are now visible to your right, and you are aware of traffic noise from the A286 Chichester-Midhurst road. The path enters a small cutting, goes under a bridge and then shortly beyond that bridge passes under the A286 bridge. Just beyond the A286 bridge is some modern housing to your left, and amongst this housing is a tall quite distinctive building that is the redevelopment of the old Lavant station building. There is no possibility of access into the building, it being now a private dwelling.

The pedestrian/cycle track is temporarily halted here for about half a mile, although even along this half mile you can remain reasonably close to the course of the old line. When the trusty metalled path comes to an abrupt halt beyond the new development round the old station, don't be tempted to swing left to join the road, but go forward onto a long narrow strip of grass, following the same line as the old railway. The scene to your right is most pleasant, with the river Lavant, active during most winters, below you to your right, and splendid rolling countryside beyond. You pass a children's play area, also to your right, and beside which you have to dodge round a barrier, but you can continue along the grassy strip beyond it; directly ahead is housing, and the course of the old line is now completely lost in this comparatively new residential development. When you reach the housing, bear to the right of No. 97 "Riverview" to briefly follow a metalled path beside the river, but you are soon forced left, away from the river, along a concrete drive to a residential road. Turn right to follow this road. The houses to your right are built along the course of the old line, and you can only imagine what a lovely view passengers would have had across the river to the beautiful countryside to the east, including the masts on the well-known hilltop beauty spot known as the Trundle. You pass three turnings which go off to the right, namely St Roche's Close, East View Close and St Mary's Close. The road bends left; just before the left bend is a small crescent which at the time of writing bore no signboard, and you need to take the first of the two offshoots, walking diagonally across the green, and aiming for the roadway leading off between no. 15 and no. 17. Go forward to a Centurion Way information board to find yourself on the course of the old line again, much of which, as far as West Dean, has been converted into another stretch of pedestrian/cycle track. Looking back at the houses you are leaving behind, you will see the impossibility of following the line between Lavant station and this point!

This next section of the Centurion Way which you now follow as far as Binderton, is if anything even more rewarding than the stretch between Chichester and Lavant with its splendid scenery, the A286 providing a constant but not too intrusive companion to your left as you proceed onwards. You soon cross two bridges over watercourses, one being the river Lavant and the other being a tributary; in winter both streams are likely to be very full and make an extremely picturesque sight. There are still delightful views to the Trundle on your right, and to Kingley Vale Nature Reserve on your left, and one other very attractive feature of this section is the line of trees on each side of the path. Beyond the line of trees you continue through lovely open countryside, approaching what is the first overbridge since just before Lavant station, and just before the bridge (1), the Centurion Way goes off to the left.

Now you have a choice. The next section of old line isn't along a designated right of way, and there is an obstruction in the form of a locked gate, so really you should seek permission to walk it and surmount the gate (please refer to my introductory notes). If you are going to carry on along the old line, go through the gate which provides access to the continuation of the old line under the bridge; continue along the old line, passing through two sets of metal gates with farm sheds bordering the old line, and the converted farm buildings of Farbridge just over to the left. Beyond the second set of gates, go forward to cross over a track and continue on the old line along rougher ground, effectively a left-hand field edge. At the corner of the field further progress appears impossible, with fencing and trees immediately ahead, but there is a crude stile over the barbed wire; cross over it with care and bear briefly left into what is a narrow strip of vegetation between fields, then bear right to emerge from the strip into a field, and

A lovely section of the Chichester-Midhurst walk immediately to the west of Chichester.

simply follow the right-hand field edge round, very shortly now able to access the old line again to the right. It is now very easy walking along a clear stretch of old line, with lovely views to the West Dean estate, again to your right. It's along here that you will meet the metalled gate which was locked at the time of writing, and having negotiated it, you continue along the old line, soon arriving at the A286 overbridge crossing (2); this is an impressive construction, feeling more like a tunnel than an overbridge. If you decide not to follow the section of old line beyond (1), you need to walk up the Centurion Way beyond (1) to arrive at the A286 and turn right to follow beside it until you cross the old line using the overbridge crossing at (2) above. Just beyond the crossing, you can turn left off the A286 to access the course of the old line.

Follow the old line now towards the West Dean Tunnel, passing the charming village of West Dean. The surrounding countryside is quite delightful; note the attractive grouping of flint buildings to your left and a particularly fine flint and brick house to your right just beyond the bridge over the West Dean-Staple Ash Farm road. Not far beyond this underbridge, you reach the mouth of West Dean Tunnel, the first of three big tunnels on this route, but in common with the other two, it is not open to the public. It being impossible to climb the cuttings just short of the tunnel, retrace your steps along the old line almost back to the A286 overbridge, but just beyond the sports field, turn left along a track to arrive at the A286 and bear left to follow this road, using the pavement to the left. There is a welcome pub, the Selsey Arms, at the bottom of the hill on the other side. Walk up the hill beyond the Selsey Arms, and, level with the start of the woodland on the left, turn left onto a signed footpath through the trees. There is shortly a fork junction; by a detour along the left fork you can get a good view of the tunnel mouth from above, but to progress you need to take the right fork and then take the next right turn beyond that. Almost immediately there's a clearing to the right, with two tracks leading away from it, an upper and a lower track. You need to bear right into the clearing then take the upper of the two tracks, proceeding left (north-eastwards) through the trees, and soon you'll be aware of the old line emerging from the tunnel to your left. You drop down and arrive at a T-junction with a lane, the old line crossing the lane just to your left; you can't join the old line beyond this lane, so turn right to follow the lane down to the A286. Turn left to follow the A286 briefly, but very soon - just a few yards in fact - you reach a lane on the left signposted Colworth Farm (3).

Now you have another choice. You could bear left up this lane, go under the bridge and, leaving the lane to the right, scramble up the bank to join the old line which can be followed from here all the way on to the old Singleton station, but there are a pair of wooden fences - marking the next underbridge - which have to be surmounted. If you're not happy about crossing these fences, carry on past the Colworth Farm lane at (3) above and take the next turning on the left, soon turning right into a playing field, at the top corner of which you can scramble up onto the old line beyond the wooden fences. The two routes are now reunited and it's easy going along the old line all the way to the old Singleton station. This building did look very sorry for itself at the time of writing, but the views to Singleton village and the adjacent Weald & Downland

One contented canine enjoying the Chichester-Midhurst walk just north of Lavant.

museum are excellent. Keep on the old line beyond the station, until you find your way ahead blocked; at this point you need to bear right to follow the left-hand field edge parallel with the old line, then at the far corner of the field you can go forward over some modest undergrowth to reach a public footpath. Turn left to join it. Don't cross the old line by the path, but bear right just before the crossing to drop down - quite easily - to the old line. It's easy to follow but all too soon the way forward is blocked by a fence and vegetation, so you should turn left and then follow the right-hand field edge keeping the old line parallel with you to the right.

Keep descending along the field edge, then at the bottom veer right to pass under the old line, bear left and follow the left-hand field edge up to a point where you're level with the old line and there's an opening to allow you to cross it. Accordingly, cross over here to the next field and bear right to follow the right-hand field edge, parallel with the old line cutting which is to your right, and able to observe the southern mouth of Singleton Tunnel. Follow the field edge round, veering left and then right, keeping the woods to your right; soon after veering right, use the stile to enter the woods on the right and immediately join a track. Very shortly you reach a T-junction of tracks, where you turn left and follow a clear track quite steeply downhill to another T-junction. Turn right but then turn almost immediately left along a signed National Trust path which goes uphill and arrives at a T-junction; turn right here and you'll soon find yourself able to look left at the northern mouth of the Singleton Tunnel, the old line a long way below you! Follow the National Trust path on to shortly reach a crossroads of paths, and here turn left to walk along a clear path downhill, keeping the old line cutting parallel with you to the left. You arrive at yet another T-junction of paths and it's possible to bear left to join the old line here; in fact you can backtrack along the old line to the northern mouth of the tunnel and I do recommend you do so, as it is extremely scenic and not difficult to negotiate. Retrace your steps and now go forward along the old line, unfortunately soon being forced to drop down to a footpath which skirts the buildings of Littlewood Farm, turning right onto this path.

You now (4) have a further choice which will be determined by your ability, or inability, to access and proceed beside the land around Littlewood Farm. To stay as faithful to the old line as possible, you need to bear immediately left up a farm road towards the farm outbuildings on the far side of the course of the old line - it is prudent to seek permission to do this - but immediately after crossing the old line bear right to follow the right-hand field edge, walking parallel with the old line which is to your right. The old line now starts to dip down into a cutting and is very difficult to follow, so don't bother to try and drop down to follow it; rather stay immediately above it and when you reach the woodland, go straight on into it, keeping the old line below you to the right. It is now possible to walk through the woodland immediately above the cutting - progress is generally straightforward - and shortly you reach another footpath crossing, actually a farm track, just above Wolverstone Farm. If you are unable or unwilling to follow this route, walk on from (4) down the path to reach the A286 and turn left to follow beside

it to the Wolverstone Farm buildings, turning left again onto a clear gated track. Walk through or round the gate and over the course of the old line, to be reunited with the first choice route.

From the Wolverstone Farm track, however you've arrived at it, take a track leading away from it to the north just beyond the overbridge crossing of the old line, but then immediately bear right off that, and walk through the thick woodland parallel with the old line which is below you to your right. Keeping as close to the top of the cutting as you can, descend gradually, forging a path between the trees, to arrive at the old line, crossing over low fencing to access the line itself. Progress isn't easy, and you need to be patient as

Two peaceful sections of the Chichester-Midhurst walk near Binderton, popular with both walkers and cyclists.

you make your way along, with a number of obstructions in the form of fallen trees. Keep to the left side of the course of the old line, and look out very carefully firstly for a crude path rising gently from the old line on the left, but staying immediately beside it; take this path which, very narrow in places, rises from the old line and emerges from the woods into an area of rough grass. Now proceed along the grass, keeping the old line close to your right but with an increasingly steep cutting separating you from it, while there's a clear track now parallel with you to the left. In due course you arrive at the southern mouth of Cocking Tunnel; you should not attempt to drop down to the tunnel mouth, and signs warn you against trying to enter the tunnel itself. Join briefly the path just to your left here and almost immediately arrive at a clear track coming in from the right. Turn right onto this track, look down at the old line again as it enters the tunnel, then follow the track to the A286 and turn left to walk beside this road to its junction with the South Downs Way a couple of hundred yards ahead. Turn left again here to briefly join the South Downs Way. You can save yourself a few yards of roadside walking by cutting through the popular Cocking Hill car park just to the left of the A286, turning left onto the South Downs Way at the top end of the car park.

You follow the South Downs Way for just a few moments, turning right just before the farm buildings down a path indicated by a fingerpost as "Public Right Of Way". The path drops quite steeply and swings left; as it does so, turn right off the path and walk through the trees then down the side of the bank to arrive back on the old line. Just to your right here is the northern mouth of Cocking tunnel. This is one of the best spots on the whole walk: a marvellous combination of impressive railway engineering and beautiful unspoilt natural surroundings. Please note that the tunnel is now protected by a metalled fence and can't be entered, but looking down it you can see the light at the other end of the tunnel and imagine the drivers of the many trains passing through it. You can now follow the old line northwards towards the old Cocking station. The going is initially quite easy with lovely views to the Downs on both sides, but it becomes rougher, so be careful. You emerge through the thick undergrowth onto firmer grass, and find your way ahead obstructed by a fence beyond which is the old station at Cocking, now a private dwelling. Bear left through a gate to arrive almost immediately at a track; turn right and follow this track which takes you alongside the green embankment on which the line was built, past the old station platform and the magnificent station building. Just beyond the building you reach a T-junction with the Cocking-Bepton road onto which you turn right, then pass under the old railway bridge. If you wish to detour to the village of Cocking with a very good range of amenities for a small village - shop, pub and café! - just continue along the road to its end, but the railway walk bears left off the road shortly beyond the old railway bridge, turning hard left up a little slope to a gate beyond which is a sports field. You can cross the field to return back to the course of the old line and scramble through the trees to walk onto the bridge you've just passed underneath. However the vegetation is too thick to proceed direct along the line so return to the sports field and now follow its left-hand edge, walking to its top left-hand end and continuing forward, keeping to the right of the old line and walking along the left edge of the next field. Very shortly you're able to join the old line again.

You're now able to follow the old line for the best part of a mile. The going is generally quite easy, with not too many obstructions, although you do have to negotiate two collapsed bridges over lanes coming down from the A286, of which you're constantly aware because of the traffic noise. The first collapsed bridge is quite easy to get round, but the second is rather more challenging and indeed beyond the second collapsed bridge the going is definitely harder. You then come to a third collapsed bridge: not only will you need to take great care in scrambling down to the crude path at the bottom, but there's no way of being able to regain the old line on the other side. You need to bear left along what is an ill-defined path that goes parallel with a stream and arrives at a public footpath just by the attractive Pitsham Place. Turn right onto the footpath and follow it, as signed, keeping Pitsham Place to your left and going forward to a metalled lane with good views to the old line on the right. Soon you reach a junction with Pitsham Lane and here turn right. You soon reach the old line again, and there is a path leading up to a gate which would appear to give access to the old line itself, but don't bother to surmount it; beyond the gate is a field in which horses are kept, and there is no way out of the field at the other end. Therefore continue along Pitsham Lane to arrive at the A286, turn left and follow the road. Fortuitously, just as with the section of A286 you had to follow at West Dean, you reach a pub (the Greyhound) within a few yards, and you don't even have to cross the road for this one! Shortly beyond the pub, turn hard left onto a signed path, actually a lane to begin with, which soon passes underneath the old line by a particularly impressive brick bridge. There is no way of accessing the old line on either side of the bridge. The only ascent unprotected by fencing is on the nearside to the right, but it is far too steep, and even if you did make it to the top, the way forward is thick with vegetation and, much more alarmingly, soon reaches a very steep drop which could all too easily be missed, with potentially fatal results. Therefore continue along the lane, bearing left as signed to pass a picture-book cottage along a delightful narrow stream-side path to reach a meadow. Turn right into the meadow but very shortly look left for a stile, and climb gently to cross the stile then continue westwards over the field, aiming for another stile. Cross over into a further field and go on to a third stile, beyond which you bear right as signed along a track, going forward into what is a continuation of Pitsham Lane.

Follow the clear farm track just east of north, passing a large field which is to the right, and beyond which you reach the outskirts of Midhurst. You pass a parking area/depot and then a terrace of houses which again is to your right, beyond which is a residents' parking area and immediately beyond that, a metalled road leading off, also to the right. Follow this metalled road which reaches a T-junction with a wider road, turning left onto this road and following it to its junction with Holmbush Way, turning right to follow Holmbush Way. You pass through the industrial estate - no pavement is available

- and continue straight ahead into Barlavington Way, proceeding as far as number 20 on the right-hand side, beyond which is a concrete pathway. Turn right to follow this pathway and you'll find yourself on a back alley behind the houses; immediately beyond the back alley and running parallel with it is the old line, and beyond the old line is woodland and attractive countryside. You are barely a quarter of a mile from where you last saw the old line, just beyond the Greyhound pub, so you've not missed much! Note, however, that the course of the old line is inaccessible and there's no way of joining it. Having walked as far up the alley as you can, retrace your steps along the alley and back down Holmbush Way, now in fact following the course of the old line. Note how as the road swings from north-west to north-east, so did the line; you will see in a few moments how the old line then swung south-east to arrive at Midhurst station. At the end of Holmbush Way, turn right onto the A286 and pass the fire station, just

Trespassers not welcome - the fenced-off mouth of the Cocking Tunnel on the Chichester-Midhurst line.

beyond which on your right is a stream and evidence of a railway embankment on each side of it. Continue briefly up the A286. At a sharp left-hand bend turn right into Bourne Way, soon arriving at the T-junction which marked the Midhurst LBSCR station (which was also on the Pulborough-Petersfield line - see walk 3 below) and the terminus of the Chichester-Midhurst line. By turning right at the T-junction you can see the site of the last couple of hundred yards or so of the old line, but the housing development has destroyed all traces. Your railway walk is at an end. If you want to explore the delightful town of Midhurst with its many amenities and refreshment opportunities, return to the A286 and turn right onto it, then shortly bear left down Chichester Road, going forward into South Street. This brings you into North Street, Midhurst's main thoroughfare. The bus stand is at the north end of North Street on the right.

WALK 3 - **PULBOROUGH TO PETERSFIELD**

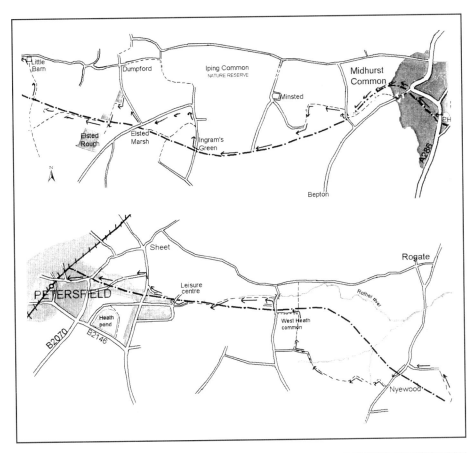

The overbridge crossing of the Pulborough-Petersfield line near Shopham Bridge.

WALK 3 - **PULBOROUGH TO PETERSFIELD**

Length:	24 miles.
Start:	Pulborough station.
Finish:	Petersfield station.
Public Transport:	Regular trains serving Pulborough on the Chichester-Arundel-Horsham-London Victoria line: regular buses (SC) from Midhurst to Chichester and Haslemere; regular buses (CL Mon-Sat, SC Sun) between Petersfield and Midhurst; regular buses (SC) between Midhurst and Pulborough; regular trains serving Petersfield on the London Waterloo-Haslemere-Portsmouth line.
Refreshments:	Fittleworth (P); Heath End (P,C); Selham (P); Midhurst (P,S,C); Elsted (P); Petersfield (P,S,C)..
Conditions:	This is a long and challenging walk, and will require two days to complete. Amenities are scarce, and you will have to detour off route for shops. It is however an immensely rewarding walk, through beautiful countryside. Several sections of the old line can easily be walked, but only one of these is on a designated right of way, and there are a number of stretches where the course of the old line is wholly inaccessible.

History

The Pulborough-Petersfield line, built during the railway boom in the mid-19th century, was opened in three stages. The first section to open was between Hardham, just beyond Pulborough, and Petworth on October 15th 1859. The section between Midhurst and Petersfield was opened next, on September 1st 1864. The section that linked these two strands, from Midhurst to Petworth, was the last to open, on October 15th 1866. The London, Brighton & South Coast Railway (LBSCR) built the sections between Hardham and Midhurst, and the section on to Petersfield was constructed by the London & South Western Railway (LSWR). Initially it was not possible to run through trains between the LBSCR-owned and the LSWR-owned sections because the connecting line across the Bepton Road bridge at Midhurst was capable of carrying only the weight of a single wagon. There were therefore two stations at Midhurst, one providing services eastwards via Selham, Petworth and Fittleworth to Pulborough and

Horsham, and one offering services westwards via Elsted and Rogate to Petersfield. It was not until 12th July 1925, after the two companies had been incorporated into the Southern Railway, that the Bepton Road bridge was replaced, the LSWR station was closed, and through services became possible. Not all the stations opened at the same time. Selham station, a simple wooden building with one platform, opened in 1872 and Fittleworth station, another modest construction with wooden canopy, in 1889. Petworth station was a grander affair, blessed not only with a large and generously canopied station building - replacing, in 1890, a squat timber structure - but also a goods yard and goods shed as well as a small locomotive shed and signal box. The station was actually a mile and a half from the town of Petworth itself, but at least there was a watering-hole immediately adjacent to the station, known as the Railway Hotel in the line's early years; there is still a pub there today. The fact that buses were able to travel conveniently to Midhurst from the centre of Petworth must have been a significant disincentive to use the train. In September 1959 a pair of circus elephants travelled by train to Petworth and had to be walked into town, hence a bicycle lamp being attached to the forehead of one of them! West of Midhurst with its two stations, there were just two intermediate stations: Elsted, over a mile north of the village of the same name, and Rogate, known also as Rogate for Harting and situated a mile and a half from each place in the village of Nyewood where there was an important brickworks. During World War 2, Rogate station was staffed by a Joan Gibbs whose duties included issuing tickets, signalling, arranging for sufficient quantities of freight transport, sheeting wagons with tarpaulins and tending the station garden. Just about the only job she did not do was cleaning out the gentlemen's toilets!

Initially the LSWR section offered five return journeys daily, but by 1913 the number had increased to eleven, reducing to ten by 1922. The LBSCR route from Hardham to Petworth also provided five return journeys in its early years, increasing to eight on extension to Midhurst. When through trains became possible, a large number of journeys still started and ended at Midhurst. The 1938 timetable shows seven trains between Pulborough and Midhurst and eight between Midhurst and Petersfield, but only two through services daily (none on Sundays) between Pulborough and Petersfield with a journey time of 51 minutes, and just one (curiously, two on Sundays) between Petersfield and Pulborough. The 1942 timetable saw a significant increase in the number of through trains. A number of trains running from Pulborough to Midhurst continued on to Chichester via Cocking, Singleton and West Dean, and there was one remarkable train which for some years left Brighton at 6.25am and proceeded to London Victoria via Chichester, Midhurst, Petworth and Pulborough, giving a journey of 101 miles! Freight conveyed on the line included not only elephants (see above) but also coal, grain, sugar, milk, bricks and timber. One of the proudest moments of the life of the line was on December 6th 1899 when the Prince of Wales and his suite travelled to Petworth by Royal Special Train; the train left London Victoria at 4.28pm and arrived in Petworth at 5.57pm. A less happy event was on 16th June 1937 when halfway between Petersfield

The splendidly restored Petworth station on the Pulborough-Petersfield line.

and Rogate a locomotive and its carriage left the rails, but fortunately there were only three passengers on board, and none of them were injured. The line, like the Selsey Tramway, prided itself on the personal service it offered to its patrons, and a number of former passengers recall acts of kindness, such as holding a train to allow a pram to be placed in the guard's van, and locating a precious dress cap which had been blown off a passenger's head and out into the countryside. There were also some amusing incidents, such as the occasion on which a family which had used the line to travel to Petersfield were delayed on the homeward train because the engine had gone off without the carriages.

After World War 2 there was a steady decline in passenger usage, due largely to the competition from the roads, with many trains running empty. British Railways, which came into being in 1948, claimed to be losing £31,000 per year on the service. Passenger trains ceased throughout on 5th February 1955, as did goods services between Petersfield and Midhurst. Goods yards east of Midhurst closed gradually over time, with Petworth being the last to close on 20th May 1966. Ironically, Midhurst station saw more people than possibly ever before for the last day of passenger operations on the line to Petersfield, and it was reckoned that only Bank Holidays prior to the First World War had seen so many crowds.

Walking the Line

Your walk begins at Pulborough station. Descend the station approach road to the village street and turn left, soon reaching a roundabout with the A29 signposted to the right; turn right to follow the A29, soon crossing over the River Arun, and continue alongside it. You pass the village of Hardham and, a short way beyond the road leading off to Hardham church on the left, turn right off the A29 along a narrow road which crosses the railway and passes a pumping station. Just beyond the railway turn left onto a signed footpath which initially follows a driveway then shortly swings left to arrive at a gate. Go through the gate and turn right; you are now on the old line only a few yards from where it branched off the still existing Pulborough-Arundel line, and you may see trains plying this route as you begin.

It's now possible to follow the old line along what has been designated a right of way, for about a mile. The scenery is delightful, with woodland to your left and the picturesque Rother valley to your right. You reach the end of the right of way section along the old line, further progress being obstructed by a gate; turn right just before the gate to walk along a footpath which heads away from the old line through the trees, crossing over a stile. As you emerge from the trees do not continue along the path as directed by the sign, but turn left to cross over the field (or round the left-hand edge of it, if crops are growing in it), aiming just to the right of the barn you can see ahead, following the (overgrown) course of the old line with your eyes. Near the top corner of the field you'll be able to rejoin the old line, turning right to follow a clear and unobstructed track, and although this track peters out you can continue ahead along the course of the old line. Initially it is easily negotiable but then becomes difficult to follow as a result of fallen trees and undergrowth; it's better early on to keep to the embankment to the left, but as that too becomes difficult to follow, you can cross to the embankment to the right and pick up a path which follows that embankment, gradually dropping back to the course of the trackbed as the obstructions diminish. Now it's a simpler walk on to an overbridge crossing, the B2138 Bury-Fittleworth road. Pass under the bridge but there's a private house and garden ahead - actually the old Fittleworth station - so you need to turn left immediately beyond the bridge and, enjoying the view to the nicely restored station, climb up to meet the road.

Turn right to follow the B2138 briefly, then take the first right-hand road turning, a minor road signposted to Coates. In a couple of hundred yards, just past a prominent house to the right, the road starts to descend, and as it does so, turn right off the road along a rough track beside the right-hand field edge; by following the field edge along the track and then round to the left, you will find yourself following parallel with the old line which is in a cutting below you. It is not feasible to join the old line just here, so continue walking parallel with the old line along the right-hand field edge, then at the bottom of the field, veer left to return to the road. Turn right to follow the road which now goes gently uphill, and at the top of this small rise there is an opening to the right, giving access to a field. Turn right to follow the right-hand field edge, heading first eastwards and then northwards, and at the north-east corner of the field you can easily access the old line and turn left (westwards) to follow it, going forward onto a clear track. This is very attractive walking indeed, with good views to the Rother valley to the right. As you approach the buildings of the little village of Coates, the track bends to the left (1). Your way is round to the left, up to the road, but by going straight ahead at the left bend, under the tree, you could detour along the course of the old line; in summer, when the trees and vegetation are at their most leafy and lush, the way ahead along the old line won't be necessarily that obvious. You have to be careful because very shortly there's a short steep drop and then a climb up the other side, but once you've got past that, the going is reasonably clear for a couple of hundred yards or so. Unfortunately, you do then reach impenetrable vegetation and you're forced back to (1) above, turning right to walk back to the Coates road.

Turn right onto the road which has now arrived at Coates. The road passes the very attractive houses of the village and then swings left; shortly beyond this left bend, look out for a signed path going off to your right, and follow this path, getting good views to line to your right. The path heads initially just north of west then descends, coming within sight of buildings straight ahead, and you need to take the wide track that veers to the left of the buildings, aiming for and arriving at the northern fringe of an area of woodland. Sight of the old line is lost as you follow the footpath, now a good track, along the northern edge of the wood. A further area of wood comes in from the right; at the junction of tracks at this point keep to the right-hand one (half-right, not another crude path going off hard right here), shortly emerging from the wood and reaching a junction of footpaths. Take the right-hand one which climbs quite steeply, keeping the wood to the right. As you climb, reaching what is a mini-summit (there is a further brow beyond), you will see a path veering away to the right here and you need to bear right along it, parallel to but some way above the wood you've just emerged from, which is on your right. You enter a field and can follow a clearly signed path which proceeds downhill; the line of vegetation straight ahead of you at the bottom of the hill marks the course of the old line. Drop down to meet and cross the old line and go forward to the river bank and a junction with a permissive path coming in from your right which follows the bank of the Rother. Your way is forward to the road crossing of the Rother known as Shopham Bridge. However you could, if you wished, detour to the right along the Rother-side path to get a better view of the course of the old line which you lost on your walk from Coates. That said, there is no way of accessing or following the old line itself as it is shrouded in robustly fenced bushes and trees, so when you feel you've seen enough, walk back beside the Rother and go forward to Shopham Bridge. Turn left onto the road to arrive almost at once at a bridge crossing of the old line.

It is possible to scramble down the bank just beyond the bridge and turn left to join the old line here, and if you are feeling adventurous and either have planned carefully or are very lucky, it MAY be possible for you to follow it all the way to Petworth station. Progress is easy enough to begin with as you follow what is a clear track, but then becomes harder as you have to negotiate a couple of gates and fencing, going forward through a field where the course of the old line then becomes indistinct. You continue through a field, carefully keeping a straight line, the ground rising just to your left; you need to aim for the very far end of the field where a stile takes you into woodland and the course of the old line becomes clear again, albeit the going is extremely rough, with many fallen trees to negotiate. You emerge into an industrial estate, and if either you have permission of the owners (at the time of writing, Hamilton Construction Services) or get lucky, it MAY be possible for you to go forward through the gates, out of the estate and forward to the old Petworth station. However, it should be emphasized that none of this walk from Shopham Bridge is on designated rights of way and progress could be frustrated by any one of the various obstructions, including the exit gates from the estate being locked; worse, if found on the industrial estate without permission, you could find yourself in trouble with the owners. If you decide to chance it, you do so at your own risk. You really are strongly advised to seek permission to walk through the estate, and if it is not forthcoming, to consider shortening your walk along the old line from Shopham Bridge and using the alternative route described below.

If you are forced back, or you decide not to attempt this direct route to Petworth station, continue briefly south-westwards along the road beyond Shopham Bridge past the old railway bridge, and very shortly you will see a signed path going over a stile to your right. Go over the stile and immediately turn left to follow the path which goes uphill along the left-hand edge of the field, parallel with the road. You reach the top left-hand edge of the field and here bear right, keeping the wood to your left and the field to your right. Continue until you reach, shortly, a signed footpath going off left into the wood, then follow the path through the wood downhill to arrive at a road with the delightful Burton Mill Pond beyond. Turn right to follow the road, continuing north-westwards along the road for about three quarters of a mile, then bear right onto a footpath opposite the left turn signposted Burton Park Farm. Follow this path which soon veers gently left and

The old Selham station building on the Pulborough-Petersfield line.

43

passes through woodland to arrive at the A285 at Heath End; turn right onto the A285 and follow it downhill until you reach the Badgers pub on the right-hand side. Just before the pub, turn hard right onto an approach road which leads to the old Petworth station where you're reunited with the more direct route from Shopham Bridge. The station building has been magnificently restored, and at the time of writing offered not only bed and breakfast accommodation but refreshments too. It would certainly be a delightful break from your walking endeavours to stop for tea and cake and admire not only the interior of the station house but the splendid Pullman coaches adjacent to it. (Remember that Petworth station is a good mile and a half away from Petworth itself.) However you have reached the old station, make your way to the A285 by the approach road; the Badgers pub - another delightful refreshment opportunity! - is to the right, but you need to turn left to follow the A285 very briefly. Walk up to just short of the bridge over the old line, reaching a signed public right of way going off along a lane to the right, and you now follow this lane until you reach a house on the right-hand side, no more than a few hundred yards along. Across the track from the house is a gate leading into a field; turn left through the gate and go across the field to a gate at the far end. The way across the field is not a designated right of way but there was no difficulty of access at the time of writing. The gate (2) at the end of the field may be open, but equally it might not be, and it isn't a sturdy construction; you must avoid any risk of damage to it, and you may prefer not to take the risk. If all is well, simply go through, past or over the gate and turn right to find yourself on the course of the old line, skipping the directions given in the italicised paragraph below. Otherwise, you'll need to refer to the directions given in the italicised paragraph.

If you decide not to risk the gate, you'll need to backtrack all the way to the A285. Turn right to follow the road uphill, reaching a garage premises with long stone buildings just beyond them; immediately past these buildings turn right onto a signed bridleway. Follow the bridleway which passes some houses and goes forward into woodland, leaving the houses behind. Soon after entering the woods you pass a track going off to the right, then you drop downhill, going over a path crossing and soon afterwards arriving at a multi-path junction, with a signed footpath going off to the left; you need to stick to the main path, rising and keeping a large field immediately to your right. When you arrive level with the top left corner of the field you pass a bridleway sign pointing in each direction, and at this point, you reach a crossroads of paths where you need to turn right, keeping the west side of the field to your right. Ignoring paths going off to the right and left, follow this delightful path downhill through the woods, arriving a T-junction of paths at the bottom of the hill. Turn right here and follow the track which shortly bends left and drops downhill to arrive at the old line. While you could simply turn left to follow the course of the old line north-westwards towards your ultimate destination, you really should backtrack just over half a mile to the gate referred to at (2) above as the walking is so enjoyable - old railway walking at its best.

Although not a designated right of way, there is now, apart from a gate right at the start, an unobstructed walk along the old line virtually all the way to the next village, Selham, and it is superb disused railway walking. To begin with you are in the shade of woodland, and you can look down to the Rother to your right, then you emerge from the woods to enjoy really fine open walking through the Rother valley, the course of the old line stretching invitingly ahead of you. You pass Cathanger Farm which is to your left, and enjoy views to the pretty village of Tillington which is to your right. Continue to enjoy this section of old line until a collapsed bridge over the Selham-Fitzlea Farm track means you are forced off the old railway and down to the track; although it is possible to regain the old line on the other side, progress is shortly blocked yet again, so simply return to the farm track and follow it westwards. As you approach farm buildings, it may be possible for you to detour left through a gate into a field and follow it across to view the course of the old line from above, on its approach to Selham. However it's not possible to join the line, owing to a combination of fencing and vegetation, so retrace your steps to the farm track and continue on to the farm buildings. You pass between the farm buildings to arrive shortly at Selham, and turn left onto the little village street. You soon reach the Three Moles, which has an outstanding reputation for the quality of its beer, and which will make a delightful stop, if it is open; at the time of writing, it was open all afternoon at weekends. Beyond the pub and the collapsed underbridge crossing you could shin up the embankment to the left to view the course of the old line going back the way you've come, but it's hardly worth following. The way forward towards Midhurst along the old line definitely can't be followed, so assuming you have enjoyed a pint at the Three Moles, retrace your steps along the street and turn next left to walk along the South Ambersham road.

Soon you reach the little village church, just beside which is a signed footpath leading off to the left, and by following this path across a field, you'll arrive back on the course of the old line and can view the old Selham station building to your left. This, and the course of the old line adjacent, is private property and not accessible. It's not feasible to join or follow the old line going on towards Midhurst either, so you need to return to the road and follow it all the way to South Ambersham, consoling yourself that the road is quiet and you can follow the course of the line with your eyes, observing some embankment stretches of the old line to the left across the polo fields. At South Ambersham, turn left at the T-junction onto the Heyshott road which climbs into woodland. You pass the remains of an underbridge which carried the old line over this road, then shortly turn right onto a wooded track, which is a signed public right of way. You very soon reach a junction of tracks; the signed right of way is straight on, but you turn right here and almost at once find yourself back on the old line, bearing left here to continue along the old line towards Midhurst.

There follows an excellent stretch of walking along the course of the old line on a clear unobstructed track, albeit not a designated right of way. The track passes through beautiful woodland, but with breaks in the trees which allow views towards Cowdray Park to the north, and there's also a fine brick overbridge (3), shortly beyond which there are signed footpaths going off to the right and left. Keep on along the old line, which continues as a good wide track but then becomes a thinner path on an embankment, still in lovely unspoilt surroundings. You're then forced down off the embankment to the left, arriving immediately below and to the left of another splendid bridge (4), carrying the course of the old line forward. Providing you obtained permission, you could pass through the gate to the left just here, turning immediately right and following the right-hand field edge to another gate; beyond it, you can look onto the course of the old line which is immediately ahead of you and to the left. However, you shouldn't enter the field beyond the gate, as it is effectively a private garden turned over for various sporting activities and the road beyond is blocked off by a fence. So backtrack to the bridge at (4) above, and now make your way through the gate and under the bridge on a farm lane which passes the buildings of Oaklands Farm and goes forward to a T-junction with Oaklands Lane onto which you turn left. If you're not comfortable about passing through or over the gate by the bridge at (4) above you'll need to backtrack to just short of the fine brick overbridge at (3) above, and take the left-hand path of the two signed footpaths referred to earlier in this paragraph. You soon arrive at a T-junction of paths and here turn left. Follow the path to a sharp right-hand bend where there's a junction, and you need to carry straight on, effectively in the same direction in which you've just been walking. You rise then descend to a T-junction; turn right and then proceed to a crossroads, here turning left along Oaklands Lane to be reunited with the more direct route.

Continue along Oaklands Lane, soon passing through the village of West Lavington. You leave the village centre behind and continue along the road, with woodland to the right; as the road bends left, you will see the course of the old line coming in from the left but it is impossible to join in either direction. Just to the right (west) of here the old line having entered thick woodland plunged into a tunnel - you can see the tunnel mouth from the road - and emerged from it on the other side of the A286 Chichester-Midhurst road. You can't access the tunnel, so follow the road on to the Royal Oak pub on the right just a short distance further on, and then cut through to the A286 by means of the pub garden and car park. Turn right onto the A286 and follow this towards Midhurst, descending with the road, which bends sharply left at a junction with Chichester Road. Just beyond the sharp bend, turn left into Bourne Way and left again into The Fairway; the junction of Bourne Way and The Fairway is the approximate site of Midhurst LBSCR station. By continuing up the Fairway you can look ahead of you to the boarded-up western mouth of the tunnel referred to above. Beyond Midhurst LBSCR station, there was then an overlap between the line going on to Petersfield and the line going south to Chichester, but all traces are now removed (see chapter devoted to the Chichester-Midhurst line). To resume your Petersfield-bound journey you need to return via the Fairway and Bourne Way to the A286. However this being roughly the halfway point from Pulborough to Petersfield, it may be convenient to call a halt and seek refreshment and rest in Midhurst, easily reached by turning right onto the A286 then left down Chichester Road. To carry on along the old line towards

An attractive wooded section of the Pulborough-Petersfield line just east of Midhurst.

Petersfield, proceed along the A286 in the other direction (north-westwards). Continuing on, therefore, follow the A286 past the fire station and the Holmbush Way turning as far as a sharp right-hand bend, bearing left here onto Bepton Road. (The old Petersfield line ran along the embankment just to your left beyond Holmbush Way, its course now obscured by housing development.) Having turned left into Bepton Road, fork right almost at once into Station Road; just along this road to the left is the old LSWR station, now a commercial premises. The course of the old line is now covered by an industrial estate, and can't be followed onwards, so having joined Station Road from Bepton Road bear almost immediately right onto a signed bridlepath, and then at once bear left onto a signed footpath going roughly parallel with the road. Keep along the path, which soon bends quite sharply right and goes uphill, passing a footpath signpost. Just beyond this signpost you reach a path junction where you need to take the left fork, then look out very carefully for a path going off shortly to the left; take this left path which continues through the trees and emerges at a more open area and another path junction. This time you need to keep to the right-hand path, a clear sandy track which proceeds on through trees, now keeping the course of the old line parallel with you to the left. You arrive at a crossing of another track with a collapsed underbridge immediately to your left; go straight over along the path which keeps parallel with the obvious course of the old line - it's easier to follow with the eyes than physically join at this point - and continue to a T-junction with Severals Road, where the course of the old line becomes lost in the housing of the village of Bepton.

Bear left into Severals Road and follow it down to a parking area on the right - there's a convenient pub to your left here - and turn right by the parking area along a signed path, heading initially just south of west then veering very gently north of west to cross a field, aiming for a stile. You go over the stile onto the course of the old line and cross straight over it, there being no possibility of following it more than a short distance in either direction. Once over the old line you shortly cross a plank bridge and reach a footpath signpost, bearing half-left as directed and following the obvious if rather winding path through the woods. You reach at a T-junction with a driveway and turn left onto it, proceeding past a gateway towards an impressive house; as the driveway bends left just before the house, look out for and take a signed path going right which follows the left-hand edge of a pleasant green, arrives at a stile and goes forward to another driveway. Turn left to follow this driveway briefly, but as it shortly bends right (a signpost pointing the footpath in that direction), leave the driveway and follow a rougher track in the same direction as you have just been walking. This track could be quite overgrown, and indeed you will have to clamber through undergrowth as you veer left to aim for a field, the course of the old line clearly visible beyond it. You now simply walk through the field to rejoin the line, turning right to enjoy a splendid stretch of old line, nearly two miles in length, all the way to Ingrams Green Lane. Your progress south-westwards is initially rather difficult, with a lot of vegetation to negotiate, and just south of Minsted you will need to drop down the embankment to pass round a collapsed bridge, but you can pick it up again at once. The scenery is quite superb, with breathtaking views to the South Downs escarpment to your left, although you should note that none of this stretch is along designated rights of way. You will know when you've reached the Ingrams Green Lane overbridge as the course of the old line, having followed quite rough ground, joins a driveway, but this driveway veers away from the course of the old line just before the overbridge, vegetation preventing you proceeding under the bridge. Follow the driveway up to Ingrams Green Lane and turn right to join it, now being forced away from the old line.

Cross the bridge and proceed up the lane. In just under half a mile you arrive at a signed footpath going off to the left, and it is possible to view a section of old line beyond the Ingrams Green Lane overbridge by following this path just south of west to arrive at a crossing of a stream, turning sharply left here and heading southwards then south-westwards across the field beyond. However progress along the old line is impossible very far in either direction, the way ahead blocked by a stout barbed wire fence, so you would have to retrace your steps all the way back to Ingrams Green Lane. Whether you decided on the detour or not, follow Ingrams Green Lane to the next junction, then turn left into Elsted Road. Follow the road, in due course arriving at a small industrial estate - there's a convenient pub on the left as well - then turn right here into Trotton Road. Pass the buildings of Greenacre Farm, then not far beyond the farm turn left onto a footpath which follows a right-hand field edge along the left side of a patch of woodland. Keeping the woodland immediately to your right, continue along the footpath to arrive back at the old line and turn right to proceed along it, initially on the south fringe of Park Copse and then through open fields. It is not a designated right of way, but access is unobstructed until all too soon you reach another area of woodland, where the old line follows the top of an embankment and becomes difficult to follow. To make progress you need to enter the field immediately to the right of the embankment and follow the left-hand field edge parallel with the embankment almost to the (fenced) bottom end of the field. However, just at the end you can veer left to reach the old line again, easily identifiable thanks to remnants of a collapsed bridge. Turn right and scramble up onto the embankment to rejoin the old line, very soon passing a stile which is to the right and almost immediately beyond that, a stile (5) to the left.

It is now possible to follow the old line for roughly a quarter of a mile to the next junction of the old line with a footpath, marked by stiles to the right and left (6). However it is not a designated right of way and it is very rough going in parts; although there are no fenced obstructions, there are a number of fallen trees and also holes in the ground, making progress very awkward. If you don't fancy it, cross the stile at (5) above and proceed across the field south-westwards as indicated by the signpost pointing in that direction (not the one pointing along the left-hand field edge). The path is very badly defined but aim just to the right of the telegraph pole in the field, and you'll see a stile; walk to the stile and cross over into the next field, going forward to another stile and gate at the next field boundary. Cross this stile and enter a further field, walking across it to reach a signed footpath crossroads, turning hard right here to walk across the field, now heading northwards back towards the old line. You reach a stile and further field boundary, crossing the stile into the next field and bearing left to follow the left-hand field edge round. You soon reach a gate and stile in the hedge on the left; cross the stile to join a clearly signed path through a strip of woodland to reach the old line via a stile at (6) above. Whichever route you took to get to (6), it's not really feasible to continue along the old line westwards on to Nyewood from here, for although progress is initially fairly easy it becomes extremely difficult, with further extensive vegetation and falling trees posing a risk of damage to yourself or your equipment, and in any event there is physically no way through to Nyewood along the old line. So cross the stile on the north side of the old line at (6) and continue north-westwards, initially through the trees then across a stile into fields. Still observing the footpath signs, go uphill through the fields to a driveway that skirts the west end of Clarefield Copse, and follow this driveway uphill to reach Dumpford Lane; turn left to follow this road for half a mile or so to the Rogate-Harting road, and here turn left to enter the little village of Nyewood. Proceeding along the village street, you soon reach the railway bridge. Just beyond it you can detour left, downhill, to look at the old Rogate station, which has been very pleasingly redeveloped and you can walk briefly westwards to the road overbridge crossing but further progress in either direction is impossible; the old line back towards Elsted Road is barred by an industrial estate and fencing, while fencing and private gardens prevent access onwards towards Petersfield. Unfortunately, there is no acceptable way of rejoining the old line this side of West Heath Common, so you will now have to part company from it for some time. Return to Nyewood village street and continue along it in a south-westerly direction until you reach a signed footpath going off to the right opposite the phone box. Follow this path, clearly signposted, into and through an area of woodland. Emerge from the woods and continue along the footpath through a field, heading in roughly the same direction; you arrive at the edge of a strip of woodland and now bear left, along the extreme right-hand edge of the field. At the end you turn sharply right, entering a larger field and following it to its end, then bear right to enter another field briefly, going forward as signed into a further field and following it just west of north, aiming for a line of pylons. Passing just to the right of a pylon you find yourself on a track which swings sharply left round the buildings of Down Park Farm. Shortly a signed path goes off to the right. Take this path - part of the Sussex Border Path - and, ignoring a path going off to the left, follow it as signed across the very picturesque West Heath Common to be reunited with the old line at a collapsed bridge.

It is possible to backtrack beside the course of the old line along a left-hand field edge for a few hundred yards, and where barbed wire blocks further progress you could continue on round the field edge to pass through a gate then wade through bracken to join the old line. However progress back towards Nyewood is shortly completely frustrated by further barbed wire so you'll need to return to the collapsed underbridge and there is no physical problem in turning left to join the line on the west side of this bridge and following it. I say no "physical" problem because there are various signs deterring potential trespassers, including, at the time of writing, a warning that trespassers will be catapulted into space; best, therefore, to seek permission first. The

An overbridge crossing of the Pulborough-Petersfield line at Nyewood.

track along the course of the old line veers a little away from it to arrive at a T-junction with a parallel track (which can be followed from the collapsed underbridge if permission to follow the old line is not granted and you're concerned about the repercussions!), and on reaching the track you turn right to follow it to the Maidenmarsh-West Harting road, the old line easily identifiable to your right. Turn right onto the road, immediately passing what is left of the railway bridge crossing over the road.

Following the road briefly, you soon meet a narrow road going off to the left, leading to Durford Mill. Go along this road and, as the road swings right, keep on in the same direction along a path that now strikes out south-westwards across a large field. You can see the a portion of the old railway embankment to your left, but this fizzles out and the course of the old line is lost in flat fields, but you can use the location of the surviving sections of embankment to guess the route it took. Cross a stream by means of a footbridge and continue by the left-hand edge of a wood beside the banks of the River Rother, which you will recall from earlier in your walk. You follow the river for a short distance then just before reaching another patch of woodland - you can see another stretch of railway embankment through the trees - turn right over the Rother by means of a footbridge, crossing the border from West Sussex into Hampshire. You go on in the same direction, keeping a fence to your left, and reach a stile; go over the stile and now turn left (don't go straight on, as the sign suggests) to walk parallel with the fence, now heading just north of west and with the river to your left. Proceed just above the river, separated from it by a fence and an area of marsh, and arrive at another stile. Go left over the stile and descend to the river, crossing the footbridge, then beyond the bridge, swing right with the path to go briefly uphill past some bushes to arrive at an open grassy area. Ahead of you is now another stretch of railway embankment but as before you can only guess the course the line took to get there from the previous section of embankment in the woodland; it is now anonymous farmland. This next section of embankment cannot be walked on, and you will need to pass the eastern end of it, almost immediately arriving at the east end of Durford Road. Follow this road to a crossroads, with Penns Place going off to the right.

Now entering the outskirts of Petersfield, turn right to follow Penns Place, almost immediately passing the collapsed bridge carrying the old line over this road. Just beyond the bridge turn left onto a signed footpath along a tarmac drive with the centre of Petersfield stated to be a mile and a half away. To begin with you can easily identify the course of the old line on your left but you are forced away from it, keeping a large green area to your right and shortly entering Heathfield Road. Follow this down to a T-junction with Pulens Lane (B2199). Although you could detour left to inspect the remains of the old railway crossing over this road, just a couple of hundred yards or so along, your way is right at this road. Very soon you reach a bridge over a stream; cross the bridge, then go over the road and turn left to follow a stream-side path. Initially you pass through a modern housing estate, which has destroyed any evidence of the old line, but just after crossing Harting Down Road you reach another section of railway embankment. Note that the cycle track, which you need to follow, veers left here, and you continue along the track keeping the embankment to your right. Go forward to reach the junction with Marden Way, turning right onto this road and following it to a T-junction with Moggs Mead.

Two further sections of embankment remain. To get to the next, bear left into Moggs Mead, and shortly right into the cul-de-sac Lower Heyshott, following it to its end and then using an alley-way to enter Upper Heyshott. Turn right up this road which bends right and again peters out into an alley-way leading to Love Lane. Cross the road and turn left, and you will be confronted by the next portion of embankment; follow the unnamed road parallel with it to your right, soon reaching a T-junction with the B2070 Ramshill. Cross over and turn left, entering Station Road, then in a few yards, and opposite Tilbrook House, turn right along a footpath which runs parallel with and to the left of the final section of embankment. You pass under a bridge, the last piece of railway engineering you will see on this walk; please note that a lot of rubbish has accumulated under this bridge, and it is hardly the most salubrious corner of Petersfield! Having gone under the bridge turn immediately left, now keeping the embankment, which is inaccessible, to your left, and soon reaching a junction with the top end of North Road, beyond which there is no further trace of the old line. However you are now very close to the surviving London-Portsmouth line and the point where the Pulborough line met it. To get to that point, turn right up the alleyway linking North Road with the existing railway, turning first left to arrive at the top end of the Sandringham Road cul-de-sac. An alleyway soon leading off this road to the right leads to a green area where you can deduce the point at which the old and existing lines met. To get to Petersfield railway station, walk down Sandringham Road and then turn right into Station Road; the town centre of Petersfield, with its excellent range of amenities, can be reached by turning left into Winton Road shortly after joining Station Road. The station is a few hundred yards further along Station Road. To return to Pulborough by train, you would need to follow a very circuitous route via Havant and Barnham, so you may prefer to take the bus to Midhurst and change there for another bus back to Pulborough.

Negotiating fallen trees is an occupational hazard for the disused railway walker, as this section of the Pulborough-Petersfield line between Midhurst and Elsted shows.

WALK 4 - **SHOREHAM TO CHRIST'S HOSPITAL**

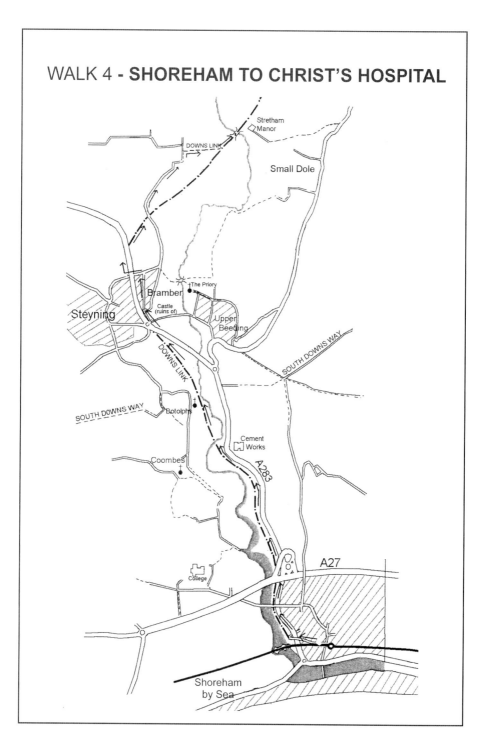

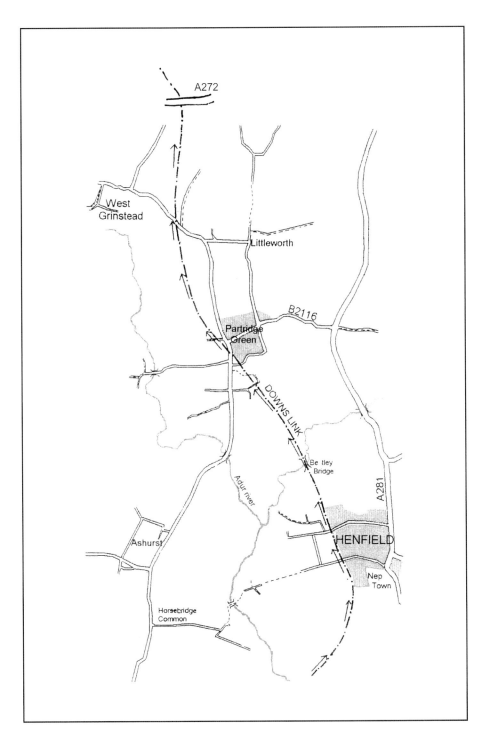

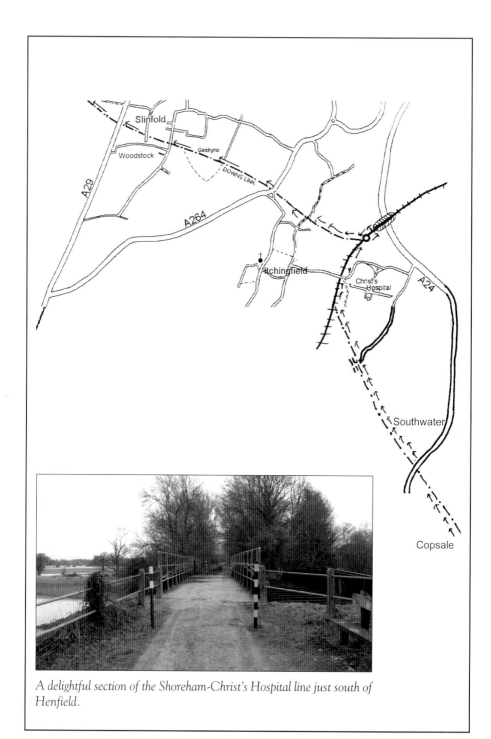

A delightful section of the Shoreham-Christ's Hospital line just south of Henfield.

WALK 4 - **SHOREHAM TO CHRIST'S HOSPITAL**

Length:	18 miles.
Start:	Shoreham station.
Finish:	Christ's Hospital station.
Public Transport:	Regular trains serving Shoreham on the Chichester/Littlehampton/Worthing/Brighton/London Victoria line; regular buses (SC Mon-Sat, CB Sun) serving both Henfield and Partridge Green on the Brighton-Horsham route; regular trains serving Christ's Hospital on the Arun Valley line between Chichester and Horsham/London Victoria.
Refreshments:	Steyning (P,C,S); Henfield (P,C,S); Partridge Green (P,S); Copsale (P); Southwater (P,C,S).
Conditions:	The majority of the walk is along the Downs Link footpath and although it doesn't follow the old line throughout, it does so for the vast majority of the route, and the whole journey is very satisfying indeed. Transport connections are excellent and amenities are never far away. It could be completed by most fit walkers in a day.

History

In the middle of the 19th century a number of schemes were mooted for a railway linking London with Brighton, although companies were deterred from proposing a direct route because of the obstruction of the South Downs. However there was a gap in the Downs, the Adur valley just west of Shoreham, and this prompted the suggestion of a line coming down to the sea via the Adur valley. Notwithstanding the fact that a direct route to Brighton, incorporating the Clayton Tunnel under the Downs, was subsequently proceeded with, real interest continued to be shown in constructing a through rail route from Horsham down to Shoreham via Steyning. Two separate railway companies, the LBSCR and SHDR (Shoreham, Horsham and Dorking Railway) put in rival bids to build the route. The LBSCR route was authorised in July 1858, linking Shoreham with the Horsham-Pulborough line (later to be extended to Arundel and known as the Arun Valley line, as it is to this day). The join was to be at Itchingfield Junction, just south-west of where Christ's Hospital station stands today, although that station didn't exist when the Shoreham line opened. The Shoreham-Partridge Green section opened in

The approach to West Grinstead; this splendid bridge carries the busy A272 over the Shoreham-Christ's Hospital line.

July 1861 and the link to Itchingfield opened two months later.

The line, which was single track to begin with but became double track in 1879, initially saw five daily trains each way, generally starting or finishing at Brighton, using the section of line linking Brighton and Shoreham that still exists today. Gradually the service increased to eleven journeys in each direction, with a much reduced service on Sundays. The summer 1948 departure shows eleven trains starting at Brighton and working the line, although the last of these, the 9.57pm from Brighton, terminated at Steyning. The first station stop out of Shoreham was Bramber, a small roadside station, then half a mile beyond came the most important station on the line for both passengers and freight, Steyning, where the weekly market adjoining the goods yard was a considerable source of traffic. After Steyning the next station was Henfield, followed by Partridge Green, West Grinstead (over a mile from the village it purported to serve) and Southwater where an adjacent brickworks brought some traffic onto the line. Itchingfield Junction was just two miles beyond Southwater, with all trains going forward into Horsham along the pre-existing line. An additional station, Christ's Hospital (named after the famous nearby school), was built just beyond Itchingfield Junction in 1902 to serve proposed housing developments which in fact never materialised. Train times between Shoreham and Christ's Hospital in 1948 were about forty-five minutes: the 9.44am, for instance, got into Christ's Hospital at 10.26am and the 4.12pm from Shoreham reached Christ's Hospital at 4.54pm.

The line enjoyed an excellent service for much of its life. In 1922 there were 10 journeys each way each weekday, every service running between Horsham and Brighton, with a total journey time between the two places of just over an hour. A commuter from Henfield to Brighton could join the 7.48am and be in Brighton by 8.26am, then catch the 5.08pm train home and be back in Henfield by 5.51pm. In 1930 there were 13 departures on the line each weekday, and this figure had risen to 17 by 1960. However passenger numbers were in decline by the early 1960's, and the line was an inevitable victim of the Beeching axe. Most freight services were withdrawn in 1962/63, and the final passenger services ran in March 1966, although some freight trains continued to run to the Beeding cement works for a time afterwards. However, as with the Christ's Hospital to Guildford line described below, the majority of the line is available for walking, the southern part of the Downs Link overlapping with it for much of its course.

Walking the Line

From the north platform of Shoreham station (for trains for Brighton and London) exit onto Brunswick Road and cross straight over into the road opposite, signed as Queen's Place. Follow this road to a crossroads junction, going straight over into Hebe Road and following this to its junction with Victoria Road. Cross over into Swiss Gardens and then turn first left into Freehold Street, taking you to a T-junction with Old Shoreham Road, just north of the point where the existing Brighton-Worthing line crosses Old Shoreham Road. Turn right into Old Shoreham Road, cross over, and follow the road north-westwards, passing a row of houses, beyond which you turn very shortly left to gain access to the old line. Although your route along the old line will proceed northwards towards the massive A27 flyover, it is possible to follow the old line almost all the way back to the point at which it left the still extant Brighton-Worthing line, and you can see exactly where the line branched off. The path back to the extant line is part of a new walkway and is initially metalled, but this metalled path veers to the right and when it does so you need to leave it and continue in the same direction along what is a rougher path, eventually reaching a dead end. Having viewed the join with the extant line, return to where you joined the old line, and now proceed northwards with confidence, following the course of the line as you will do for approximately two miles. The first section is fascinating. Immediately to your left is the Adur estuary, with views across to the magnificent Lancing College chapel, while ahead of you is the A27 flyover, and although some might regard it as an eyesore it is a magnificent piece of road engineering nonetheless.

Follow the old line under the flyover, now leaving the buildings of Shoreham behind, and continue on through pleasant but unspectacular countryside to the old Beeding cement works. You arrive at the river where you are now forced away from the old line, the bridge crossing of the river taken by the line having ceased to exist. Follow the right bank of the river upstream and in just under half a mile or so cross the river by the bridge. You are now on the South Downs Way and your arrival here signifies the start of the Downs Link, a waymarked footpath linking the South Downs Way and North Downs Way national trails. Your route will follow the Downs Link for almost all of its course. Having crossed the bridge, continue briefly up the left bank but soon arrive at a junction of paths, where you turn left to follow the South Downs Way away from the river. The picturesque church of Botolphs can be seen close by, and indeed the old line, the course of which you can clearly see coming in from the left, passed just to the east of it. Just before reaching the road beside which Botolphs Church is situated, you reach a junction of paths; you leave the South Downs Way here and turn right to rejoin the old line, using the Downs Link. You now follow the old line briefly, the Downs Link then taking you on to a path that runs parallel with it as far as the A283. The old line then proceeded to follow a route round the edge of Bramber and Steyning immediately alongside what is now the A283, and not only is there no remnant of the old stations at Bramber or indeed Steyning, but it's not practicable to follow the course of the old line past these two settlements. Following the Downs Link signposts, you cross the A283 with immense care - it is a very busy road - and walk along the Downs Link path that runs parallel with it as far as the roundabout with roads leading off to Bramber, to the right, and Steyning to the left.

Do not proceed along the A283 or turn right along the Street, but, sticking to the Downs Link, take the road between these two, Castle Lane, which initially runs immediately to the right (east)of the A283, and parallel with it. You then go straight on into Roman Road. The Downs Link turns right into King's Stone Avenue but I recommend that, in order to see another section of the old line that the Downs Link misses, and to give you the opportunity to visit Steyning, you continue all the way along Roman Road to the T-junction with King's Barn Lane. Turn left and cross over the A283 - the old line followed a course immediately beside it on the near side - then keep on along the road,

The still intact platforms and signal at West Grinstead on the Shoreham-Christ's Hospital line.

now Jarvis Lane, and veer right with the road which now becomes Cripps Lane! Continue downhill along Cripps Lane to Steyning's magnificent parish church. (If you wish to visit the lovely town of Steyning, just carry on past the church into the town centre.) Immediately before the church turn right into Vicarage Lane but very shortly reach paths going off left (into the churchyard) and right; you take the right-hand one, then in a few yards where the path widens into a road, turn left along a path which runs between areas of modern housing. You cross straight over Abbey Road and pass to the right of a children's play area, ascending to reach the A283 again. Cross straight over this road with immense care and, on the other side, descend the steps to follow a footpath that runs parallel with and to the right of the old railway embankment, carrying the old line towards Henfield. You soon arrive at a junction with a track, crossing straight over it to continue along the path, heading northwards then swinging north-eastwards, crossing a footbridge and proceeding through a field, heading uphill. Aim just to the right of the bridge where the old line passed underneath King's Barn Lane, and go forward to reach the lane; at this point you are reunited with the Downs Link. Turn left into the lane and cross the bridge, getting a good view of the course of the old line in both directions, but it isn't practicable to attempt to follow it. Simply therefore follow the lane, which soon veers right, the course of the old line over the fields to your right but impossible to discern. Proceed along the lane which you keep to until you arrive at Wyckham Farm. Note that there is a substantial building on the right a little before Wyckham Farm; don't mistake it for Wyckham Farm itself, but go past it and descend then climb gently to reach the Wyckham Farm complex. Immediately before the largest of the farmhouse buildings turn right, off the Downs Link, onto a signed footpath which leaves the farm complex and crosses a field, soon reaching a fence and veering right, then shortly veering left. Looking ahead you can now see the old line coming in to join you from the right, but inaccessible. Now keeping the course of the old line to your right, you need to follow the footpath as signed which takes you to a footpath junction immediately beside the old line; cross a stile and continue just to the left of and parallel with the old line, on a right-hand field edge. In a couple of hundred yards you reach a stile. Cross it to be reunited with the Downs Link, and bear right and almost immediately left to rejoin the old line which, using the Downs Link, you can now follow all the way to Christ's Hospital with only small breaks at Henfield, Partridge Green and Southwater.

The going is now really enjoyable as you follow the old line to Henfield; the surrounding scenery is not spectacular but it is most attractive with beautiful meadows bordering the old line and fine views to the South Downs. There is one particularly scenic spot, at the point where the old line goes over the river Adur, with the beautiful grounds of Stretham Manor immediately beyond. The scene is particularly attractive in times of very wet weather, when the fields are often flooded and this adds to the charm of the surroundings. Barely have you got into your stride, however, when you find yourself in the outskirts of Henfield; with modern development on the course of the old line, you need to bear right as signposted at the road junction, then, continuing to follow the Downs Link, you almost immediately turn left onto Station Road, going uphill to a T-junction with Upper Station Road. A useful pub is situated just across the road here. To continue along the Downs Link, turn left and shortly right onto a signed Downs Link path that immediately takes you back onto the old line, heading now for Partridge Green. However if you detour right at the T-junction by the pub, you can follow Upper Station Road, which leads into Church Street, which in turn brings you to the attractive centre of Henfield. There are ample amenities here including buses to Partridge Green and Horsham to the north, and Brighton to the south, and there are at least two cafes as well as shops and pubs. However it is quite a detour off the Downs Link, so be warned. Back on the old line beyond Upper Station Road, easy walking now takes you away from Henfield towards Partridge Green. Initially the path is in the shade of vegetation, but does open out; shortly after it does so, there is another crossing of the Adur at Betley Bridge, beyond which there is a rare section of walking over a field which can be very muddy. The countryside remains pleasant as you continue on to Partridge Green, but as you approach the houses of the village you are stopped in your tracks by a signpost pointing the Downs Link away from the old line, heading off to the left. The safer option is to follow the Downs Link which soon veers right and goes forward to follow a lane and arrive at a T-junction with what is quite a busy road, onto which you turn right and which you follow past an industrial estate (1). However, it may be possible for you to continue along the old line for a hundred yards or so, then, when further progress along the old line becomes impossible, you can bear left onto a signed footpath which then hugs the right-hand field edge and, as you reach the industrial estate, follows the estate perimeter fence. You reach a junction with a concrete driveway and then turn half-left onto a narrow path which brings you to the road at (1) above. This is quicker than the Downs Link route but at the time of writing the section of old line at the start of this alternative route was obstructed by farm waste and while it was possible to negotiate it with care, it was not easy, and the Downs Link option may be preferred. From (1) above, continue down the road to the bridge over the old line (the course of which to the right is covered by new development) then, once over the bridge, turn immediately left to follow the signed Downs Link path back down to the old line. The village of Partridge Green with good amenities and a bus link is just a few minutes' walk beyond the bridge crossing.

The going is now extremely easy all the way to Christ's Hospital, with only very minor deviations from the old line. The section between Partridge Green and West Grinstead is delightfully rural and unspoilt, with pleasant pasture on both sides and, as you approach West Grinstead, there is the very pretty Furzefield Wood to the right. You pass under a substantial bridge carrying the A272 and arrive at West Grinstead station which is one of the highlights of the walk. It has been restored to look very much as it would have done when the old line was still functioning, with platform, signal and station board, and even an old railway carriage on a piece of old railway line; there is a seat on

Going nowhere - a single railway carriage at West Grinstead on the Shoreham-Christ's Hospital line.

the platform where you can sit, enjoy a snack or a picnic, and pretend to be waiting for a train! Beyond the old station the surroundings remain very rural and attractive, with rather more woodland than previously. It is necessary to drop down to the road at Copsale, where the bridge over the road no longer exists, but there is the compensation of a lineside pub. Returning to the line, there follows a quite beautiful stretch which is best seen in the spring where the surrounding woodland is crammed with bluebells and wild garlic. Slight anticlimax follows with the negotiation of the A24 by means of a modern underpass, beyond which, remaining on the Downs Link, you follow a metalled lane running parallel with and just to the right of the old railway embankment; it is possible to detour up to the embankment but the line can't realistically be followed. You pass the remains of a railway bridge over a road to the left, Southwater Country Park just beyond, then are signposted back onto the old line which you're able to follow to Southwater itself, and as you approach a set of traffic lights, you'll see the centre of Southwater just a few yards away to the right. Although Southwater is a rather sprawling place, its centre has been rejuvenated in recent years, and even if you don't want to take advantage of the excellent range of shops and eateries there, it's worth detouring to view the magnificent modern iguanadon sculpture close to the post office.

Cross straight over the traffic lights - note the horse symbols built into the pedestrian crossing lights - and pass under the old railway bridge which is in fact the only real tangible evidence of the old railway in Southwater, with virtually all the platform now removed. Continuing along the Downs Link, follow the course of the old line to a stile, then go straight on over a field, climbing to a road; you'll see from the overbridge remains by the road that the old line has been filled in here. Beyond the road keep on the Downs Link as signed, descending and finding yourself back on the ground covered by the old line, passing another piece of bridge remains as you descend. The walking is now delightfully straightforward and rural once again, with the bonus of a path-side pub, Bax Castle, to your right. However, almost too soon you will be aware of the existing Arun Valley-Horsham-London line coming in from the left, signifying the beginning of the end of your walk from Shoreham. The Downs Link stays faithful to the old line right up to Itchingfield Junction, the point where the old and existing lines met, and then runs parallel with the existing line to within sight of a road bridge crossing just a few hundred yards short of Christ's Hospital station. You enter a wooded area along a dirt track, and it is important, just by a mileage indicator post - one of many on The Downs Link - to take the track which veers to the right to arrive at the road. Don't turn left towards the road bridge over the extant line, but go straight on over the green to the road on the far side then bear left to follow this road past the Christ's Hospital school grounds, keeping the tennis courts immediately to the right. Shortly you reach the signposted station approach road going off to the left, and it's then a short walk down to Christ's Hospital station on the London Victoria-Horsham-Arun Valley-Chichester line. Considering how busy a junction this once was, the station is now a rather modest affair with, at the time of writing, just one train an hour each way.

Christ's Hospital station, whilst the end of this walk, is the start of another superb disused railway walk which is described next. If you are wishing to go straight from one walk to the other (I do NOT recommend your trying to do all of both walks in a single day!!) don't enter the station car park but turn right just before the station sign with the traditional British Rail logo onto the driveway referred to in the first paragraph of the route description for the next walk.

Lovely woodland on the Shoreham-Christ's Hospital line approaching Copsale.

At Southwater on the northern part of the Shoreham-Christ's Hospital line.

WALK 5 - **CHRIST'S HOSPITAL TO SHALFORD**

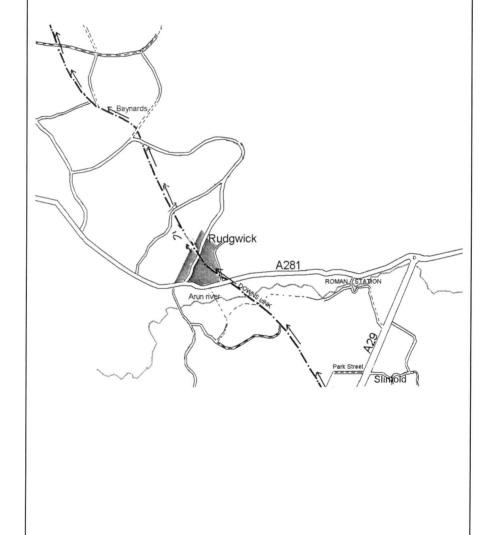

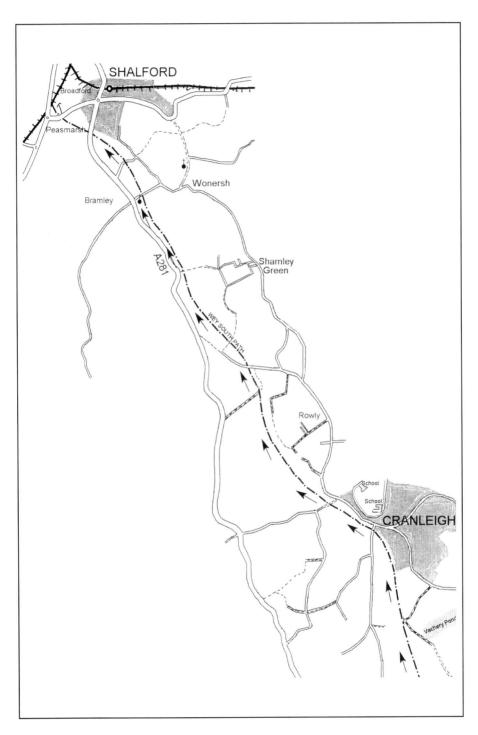

WALK 5 - CHRIST'S HOSPITAL TO SHALFORD

Length:	17 miles.
Start:	Christ's Hospital station.
Finish:	Shalford.
Public Transport:	Regular trains to Christ's Hospital on the Chichester-Arundel-Horsham-Redhill-London Victoria line; regular buses (ARR) serving Cranleigh and Shalford on the Guildford-Horsham route; regular trains serving Shalford on the Guildford-Redhill route.
Refreshments:	Rudgwick (P,S); Baynards (P); Cranleigh (P,C,S); Bramley (P,S); Shalford (P,S).
Conditions:	This is disused railway walking in its purest form, as virtually the entire route is able to stay faithful to the old line, most of it using the Downs Link footpath. It is actually even easier and more straightforward than the walk from Shoreham to Christ's Hospital which is described immediately above and is the natural "companion" walk to this. The signposting is excellent, the going is extremely easy throughout, and amenities are plentiful. Despite the high mileage most fit walkers should be able to complete this walk in a single day.

History

It was round about the time of the opening of the line linking Brighton with Horsham via Shoreham and Steyning that thought was given to a line linking Horsham with another large town, Guildford. A company known as the Horsham & Guildford Direct Railway Company duly obtained authorisation to construct a line which linked the pre-existing Horsham-Pulborough and Haslemere-Guildford lines, the new line branching off towards Guildford at Stammerham Junction, just a little short of Itchingfield Junction (see the Shoreham-Christ's Hospital chapter above) and joining hands with the Haslemere-Guildford line at Peasmarsh Junction near Shalford, two miles south of Guildford. Authorisation was given in 1860, but the LBSCR took over the line in 1864 following the bankruptcy of the contractor, and it was not until October 1865 that services finally commenced.

At the time of commencement of services, Christ's Hospital station, actually built on the site of Stammerham Junction, hadn't been opened and would not do so till 1902. Therefore the first station out of Horsham on the new branch was Slinfold, where there was a private siding to a brickworks. Shortly before the next station, Rudgwick, the river Arun had to be crossed, and the bridge crossing initially provided meant that the section of line running up to and through Rudgwick station had to be built on a gradient of 1 in 80. However, the Board of Trade would not allow trains to stop on this incline, so to achieve the prescribed 1 in 130 gradient the engineers had to raise the embankments and also the crossing of the river Arun, and this resulted in the construction of a girder bridge over the original brick arch, creating effectively a double bridge. This remains the most impressive feature of the old line. After Rudgwick the next station was Baynards, preceded by another fine feat of engineering, a 381-yard long tunnel known as Baynards Tunnel, coinciding with the summit of the line at 250ft above sea level and the crossing of the border from Sussex into Surrey. There was a goods yard at Baynards and a connection with a private rail system serving a fuller's earth plant. Beyond Baynards station came Cranleigh station, where there was a small goods yard and a siding to a gas works, and the final station prior to Peasmarsh Junction was Bramley & Wonersh. The total journey time from Horsham to Guildford was just under an hour. In 1922 there were seven weekday journeys each day between Horsham and Guildford; there was also an early morning train from Cranleigh to Horsham, going forward to London, and an early evening train from Guildford to Cranleigh plus a late Saturday night train also from Guildford to Cranleigh. A Rudgwick to Guildford commuter could pick up the 8.14am train arriving at 8.49am, with a return journey from Guildford at

A damp wintry scene on the Christ's Hospital-Shalford line near Slinfold.

The splendid double bridge near Rudgwick on the Christ's Hospital-Shalford line.

5.15pm arriving back at Rudgwick at 5.49pm. The number of daily journeys had risen to nine by 1939. In addition the line was a useful means of providing "specials," linking places which would nowadays require a most circuitous journey if undertaken by train, Surbiton to Bognor being one example. Generally, however, there were not very good connections between this line and that linking Horsham with Shoreham described above; this despite the obvious potential of Christ's Hospital, serving both lines, as a connecting station without the need to go all the way into Horsham and back out again. According to the 1948 timetable, it was theoretically possible to get a reasonable connection at Christ's Hospital if you had in mind a journey from Guildford to the coast; leaving Guildford at 10.34am you could arrive at Christ's Hospital at 11.15am and then have to wait only 8 minutes for a Shoreham-bound train. But if you missed the 10.34am the next did not leave Guildford until 1.42pm and with an hour's wait at Christ's Hospital you would not make it to Shoreham until nine minutes past four! The line led a largely tranquil existence; the most infamous incident in its line's history was on 16th December 1942 at Bramley, where a two-coach train carrying Christmas shoppers was strafed by a German Dornier 217. Seven people were killed including the guard and the driver. Perhaps it was not surprising that with ever-increasing competition from the roads, and the number of other lines serving the coast from south London and Surrey, passenger numbers decreased and, to quote H.P. White, "the line outlived its usefulness". Notwithstanding its scenic beauty - indeed it was used as the setting for a 1950's dramatisation of the film The Railway Children - it was another obvious target for Beeching, and the last train ran on 14th June 1965. However, almost all of it has been converted into a footpath/cycleway, the Downs Link following its course almost throughout, so walkers and cyclists can relive the joys of travelling on this lovely old railway.

Walking the Line

Make your way out of the booking office at Christ's Hospital and walk through the car park to join the station approach road, but almost immediately after joining it, just beyond the Christ's Hospital station sign with the traditional British Rail logo, turn hard left onto a driveway. The driveway almost immediately veers sharply left; veer left with the driveway, ignoring the pedestrian access to Christ's Hospital and also the footpath junction sign on the bend. Follow the driveway very briefly then as it veers a little more gently left, bear right onto a signed footpath with railings to the left and houses beyond the railings. You descend gently then veer left to pass under the extant Christ's Hospital-Horsham line, continuing downhill. In just under 100 yards, as the path is still descending (if you find yourself at the hill bottom, you've gone too far), look out for and take an unsigned path going off to the left through the woods. This path is not shown on maps and isn't a designated right of way, but there are no obstructions to progress. You initially rise then drop quite steeply along what is quite a thin path, before rising again and arriving at the remains of the Christ's Hospital station platform for the Shalford/Guildford branch. Note that although you're very close to the extant Christ's Hospital station "up" platform, there's no direct access from that platform to the remains, which means you're forced to take the roundabout route! As you reach what is left of the disused platform, bear right to join the course of the old line which will hardly ever be out of your sight all the way to Shalford. In less than a mile you reach Baystones Bridge; there appears to be a dead end ahead, but once you've passed underneath it you reach a Downs Link signpost. Bear left to join and walk along a path running immediately parallel to the left of the old line, now on the Downs Link.

From here it is plain sailing for several miles, as you proceed along or immediately adjacent to the old line along an excellent well-signposted path via Slinfold and Rudgwick to Baynards Tunnel. Initially the surroundings are pleasantly rural, but even when after a mile and a half you pass the housing and industrial development of Slinfold the walking remains agreeable and very easy. The old line passes a little to the south of the centre of Slinfold but there is straightforward road access to the village. The section between Slinfold and Rudgwick is in my opinion the most beautiful of the entire walk, passing lovely unspoilt woodland interspersed with fine stretches of open pasture, perhaps the climax coming with the impressive underbridge crossing of the river Arun. This bridge is quite iconic in Downs Link terms, as it forms the motif that appears on all the Downs Link signposts, but you need to drop down the steps (actually signed "View Point!") to see it properly. As stated in the introduction above, it is a double bridge, the original brick bridge not acceptable to the Board of Trade because the gradient required for the line to drop down to it would have been too great, hence the additional metal bridge built above the brick one. The scene is extremely picturesque, particularly if the Arun is swollen during times of heavy rain. Continuing on the old line beyond the double bridge, sadly the timeless atmosphere is broken with the crossing of the busy A281, beyond which the surroundings become more suburban as you approach Rudgwick. The large overbridge you reach a few hundred yards beyond the A281 carries the village street. There is very easy access to Rudgwick from the old line; look out for the Medical Centre car park to your right just beyond the overbridge, and follow the road leading from the car park up to the village street where you will find ample amenities to sustain you for the rest of your walk.

Returning to the old line, the walking immediately beyond Rudgwick is predominantly wooded and initially straightforward, but soon the marked Downs Link path is seen to fork left and go steeply uphill, the detour being necessary because Baynards Tunnel, just ahead, can't be walked through. It is quite a surprise to have such a steep climb, but the woodland walking is delightful and the reward is a lovely view to the surrounding countryside when the woodland relents. As you get towards the hilltop you arrive at a crossroads junction of paths; don't veer left with the Downs Link but take the path going effectively straight over, along the edge of the woods with an open field to your right. Initially you rise gently then start to descend and get to within sight of a road, and, as you do, look out for a path going left over a little footbridge. Take this path then very shortly bear right onto a path that goes over another little footbridge and follows along the right-hand side of the course of the old line, it having emerged from the tunnel. The cutting through which the old line went has been partially filled in here, but shortly the path is able to drop down to resume its course along the old line, passing under a bridge. Continue forward to within sight of the old Baynards station, named after the nearby Baynards Park; access to the station is fenced round so when you reach the fence you need to bear left then almost immediately right. You pass just to the left of the private but beautifully preserved station complex, and there is also a nicely sited pub just here. The need for a station here must have puzzled railway buffs even when the line was still in existence, it being apparently in the middle of nowhere and little more than a mile from the bustling village of Rudgwick. Ironically, however, it is the best preserved of all the stations on the Shoreham-Shalford route, its buildings and advertising hoardings looking very much as they would have done when the line was last operational in June 1965.

The next three and a half miles to Cranleigh along the Downs Link are very straightforward and wholly faithful to the old line. Though the beautiful woodland around Rudgwick has been left behind, the countryside remains unspoilt and attractive, with pleasant wooded walking in Lodge Copse and some particularly pleasant parkland in the vicinity of Vachery House and Vachery Pond, with a fine backdrop of wooded hills, to your right. A build-up of housing to your right and playing fields to your left signifies your approach to Cranleigh, and indeed as you pass the playing fields there's a sign pointing to Cranleigh centre, access gained by following a path just past the left side of a big leisure complex and then round the side of a car park to reach the village street. Cranleigh is an obvious place to break for refreshment, being just over halfway to Shalford and enjoying an excellent range of amenities with several food shops, pubs and cafes. There are also regular buses to Guildford and Horsham.

Returning to rejoin the Downs Link, you continue on to a road; don't go all the way up to the road junction but just short of it bear left onto a path which then arrives at the road and you then need to cross straight over the road to rejoin the Downs Link on the other side. You'll then find that progress on to Bramley along the old line is just as straightforward as it was to here from Baynards, and you have the pleasant prospect of just under 5 miles' very easy walking. It takes a while, as you might expect, to escape from the built-up area on the western outskirts of Cranleigh, but having done so you will enjoy a very pretty walk indeed, enlivened not only by the variety of scenery but by the proximity of the Wey & Arun Junction Canal, a reminder that the old railway is not the only historic form of communication in this part of Surrey. Beside the path there is a useful notice board giving information about the canal. The peace is temporarily marred by the noise of traffic on the A281 to the left but peace returns as the path veers away from the road and passes the backs of houses signifying your arrival in Bramley. If you have walked non-stop from Cranleigh, you will feel you have deserved a rest when you finally reach the road crossing that gives access to the centre of Bramley, this crossing marked by very splendid level crossing gates. If you wish to detour to the village centre, with its good range of amenities and bus links, turn left down the road and then left again at the mini-roundabout.

The well kept Baynards station on the Christ's Hospital-Shalford line.

To continue along the old line, cross straight over the road and proceed along the old and nicely kept Bramley & Wonersh station platform - note the old station signboard too - then go forward on the obvious path. The going is very pleasant, in the shade of trees, with the Wey & Arun Junction Canal keeping you company much of the way. It is on this section that you say farewell to the Downs Link which now leaves the old line and proceeds in an easterly direction to join the North Downs around St Martha's Hill. Remaining on the old line, the canal your constant companion, you will find that the sound of traffic again becomes intrusive as you approach and finally reach the A281 crossing. Pass straight over the A281 and, following a straight line, join a footpath/cycle track that continues along the course of the old line on a modest embankment. You cross over the river Wey using a comparatively recently constructed bridge, and keep on along the old line, passing under the A248 and shortly reaching a junction. A sign makes it clear that the way ahead is a permissive footpath with no public right of access, but there are no obstructions to progress and by following this permissive path you shortly reach the existing main line between Guildford and Portsmouth, and the junction between this and the old line. By continuing along the permissive path, you are now on the course of what was a proposed spur intended to link the main Guildford-Portsmouth line with the Guildford-Redhill line, and although the spur was never completed, its pleasant embankment course above the meadows is clear enough. You pass a World War 2 pillbox then descend to the river Wey, leaving the spur, the last tiny section of which, beyond the river, is inaccessible; after descending to the river, turn right to follow the Wey South Path to reach the A248 at Broadford Bridge. By turning left onto the A248 and following it you will soon reach Shalford, where there are buses to Guildford and Horsham, and trains to Guildford and Dorking.

The redundant but nicely preserved level crossing gates at Bramley towards the top of the Christ's Hospital-Shalford line.

WALK 6 - **ALDRINGTON TO DEVIL'S DYKE**

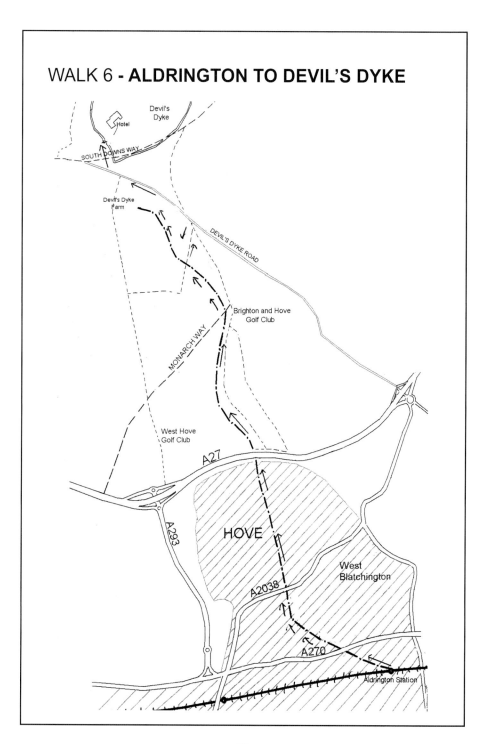

WALK 6 - ALDRINGTON TO DEVIL'S DYKE

Length:	3.5 miles.
Start:	Aldrington Station, Hove.
Finish:	Devil's Dyke.
Public Transport:	Regular trains serving Aldrington on the Worthing-Brighton line; regular buses (BH) from the Devil's Dyke restaurant/picnic area into central Brighton.
Refreshments:	Rowan Avenue (S); Hangleton Road (P,S); Devil's Dyke (P).
Conditions:	The first half of the walk is along roadsides and is relatively unrewarding. The second half is much better, offering good walking along the course of the old line or by the side of it, with fine surroundings and superb views. It is comfortably walkable in half a day.

History

Devil's Dyke has a timeless attraction, boasting magnificent views from the top of the South Downs escarpment to the Weald, as well as the extraordinary natural phenomenon which is the Dyke itself; the deep ravine is said to be the work of the Devil in his desire to flood the local communities following their conversion to Christianity. It has always been popular with visitors, and towards the end of the 19th century a company called the Brighton & Dyke Railway Company was formed with a view to creating a rail link from central Brighton - by then a bustling and popular resort - to the Dyke. The go-ahead to build the line was given in 1877 but it was not until 1st September 1887 that the line opened, following the main Worthing line to Dyke Junction (a halt was opened here in 1905, renamed Aldrington Halt in June 1932) and branching off at this junction. Although trains initially ran non-stop from Hove to the terminus, named "The Dyke" in Bradshaw's Timetable, two intermediate stations were subsequently opened on the branch to attempt to encourage further passenger usage: Rowan Halt, half a mile beyond Dyke Junction, was opened on 12th January 1934 to serve nearby housing developments, and Golf Club Halt, just under a mile from the terminus, was opened in 1891 to serve the nearby golf course. Although the line was intended chiefly for passenger use, there was a small goods yard at the terminus which received coal and cattle food and sent out hay. Station design was very basic, and the terminus was a bleak proposition indeed in winter, its location exposed and isolated.

There was normally just one staff member there, acting as booking clerk, shunter, porter and signalman! Because the branch was starting at virtually sea level and climbed to virtually the top of the downs, an almost continuous gradient of 1 in 40 was required. The 1905 timetable showed eight trains travelling to The Dyke direct from Brighton on weekdays and six on Sundays, with a usual journey time of 20 minutes for the uphill slog to the top, and just 1 minute chopped off for the descent back to Brighton. The line was temporarily closed during the First World War and closed for good on 31st December 1938. Dyke Station became a farm, and there is now no trace of any other station building.

Walking the Line

From Aldrington station take the exit on the north side and proceed down the path, turning right at the junction at the bottom then almost immediately left into Amherst Crescent. The old line left the main line very close to this point. Following Amherst Crescent up to the A270 Old Shoreham Road, you are keeping the course of the old line immediately to your left and parallel with Amherst Crescent; the site of the old line is now occupied by Sussex House Industrial Estate and is inaccessible. At Old Shoreham Road turn left, then cross over and turn right into Holmes Avenue. The old line crossed the Old Shoreham Road a fraction beyond the junction with Holmes Avenue and then swung from north-west to just west of north, through what is now another industrial estate and past the southern end of Maple Gardens. You will need to walk up Holmes Avenue and then turn left at the first crossroads, passing the cul-de-sacs of Acacia Avenue and Maple Gardens and going forward along Elm Drive. Once past the junctions with these cul-de-sacs, you are again following parallel with the course of the old line, which ran along the west side (left side as you look at it) of Elm Drive. You reach a small parade of shops, and here it's possible to bear left away from Elm Drive, soon veering right onto a path which follows the course of the old line. Sadly when the path reaches a small play area, you'll need to bear right again to arrive at Rowan Avenue (there's now no trace of Rowan Halt, the first station on the branch) turning left to follow Rowan Avenue to the junction with Hangleton Road. Cross Hangleton Road and turn left, then almost immediately bear right along an alley-way past Churchill House, following the course of the old line and arriving at a junction with West Way where you need to turn right. (The course of the old line can be followed by crossing straight over West Way into Kingston Close but there's little point in doing so as it's a dead end; if you do it, you'll need to retrace your steps to West Way and turn left.) Turn shortly left off West Way into Poplar Avenue and follow it, keeping the course of the old line to your left all the way along. Looking both back towards Rowan Avenue, and back up Poplar Avenue, and the development all around you, it seems inconceivable that there was once a railway line here! At the end of Poplar Avenue cross Hangleton Way and arrive at a signboard signifying the start of the "official" Dyke Railway Walk. Beyond the signboard, which gives a brief history of the old line, the way forward is

An excellent section of walking on the Aldrington-Devil's Dyke route.

obvious; you are now on the course of the old line, following an exceedingly good path northwards. Very soon you cross over the A27 Shoreham/Brighton bypass, then, ignoring a right fork, you continue along the path, keeping to the course of the old line. This is now quite delightful walking; at last you have left the sprawl of Brighton and Hove behind and are now in open country, with West Hove golf course immediately to your left. Looking back, you can enjoy superb views across the Brighton/Hove/Shoreham conurbation out to sea. It will perhaps only now strike you just how much height you have gained since Aldrington and how hard the engines would have had to work to haul the trains up to this height from virtually sea level. The path swings north-westwards from the A27 crossing, but then swings east of north, still sticking to the course of the old line. The going remains excellent - everything that disused railway walking should be! Having passed the northern end of West Hove golf course to your left, you now become aware of another golf course - Brighton & Hove - to your right, and the clubhouse comes into view. It is hereabouts that the old Golf Club Halt station was situated. At this point the path swings more decisively to the right, and a footpath sign points upwards past the clubhouse, away from the course of the old line. To continue along the old line you need to proceed straight on along a rougher track, in a northerly direction, rather than obeying the footpath sign. The track becomes less well defined but progress along the right-hand field edge is straightforward, with the old line just to your right and splendid views to your left. For a while it all looks very promising, but your satisfaction is short-lived because a fence ahead of you bars progress. Accordingly, just before the fence, look out for and take a green pathway to the right which crosses the course of the old line. Immediately after crossing the old line, turn left and follow the left-hand field edge round, taking great care to avoid any damage to crops especially as this isn't a designated right of way. Keeping to the field edge, now walk uphill to arrive at Devil's Dyke Road which you can join without difficulty at this point. Turn left onto the road but immediately on getting past the field boundary fence to your left, use the gate (1) to enter the field and follow the left-hand field edge down to within sight of the old line again. It's a lot of effort just to get round one fence!! Veer right at the bottom of the field to walk parallel with and immediately to the right of the old line, which you can shortly join with no obstruction and follow all the way to the site of its terminus at Dyke Farm. (None of this is along designated rights of way and if you've concerns about walking it, you may be better off simply carrying on along Devil's Dyke Road from the gate shown at (1) above and following the course of the old line with your eyes.)

On reaching Dyke Farm, there's first a gate to be surmounted, and in order to exit back onto Devil's Dyke Road you'll then need to bear right to walk through the farm complex and veer left up the farm approach road. Note, however, that there's no public right of way through the complex so it is very important to obtain permission to walk through it. If you can't obtain permission you should retrace your steps to the gate indicated at (1) above and turn left to follow Devil's Dyke Road to the top of the farm approach road. Now, whichever route you've taken, continue along Devil's Dyke Road, soon crossing the South Downs Way; you'll see the impressive ravine to your right, and shortly beyond that you will arrive at what is marked on maps as the Devil's Dyke Hotel, now an immensely popular pub and restaurant. You are now right on the edge of the South Downs escarpment and can enjoy fantastic views to the Weald, a topograph situated close by helping you to identify the places you can see from here on a clear day. There is one further feature for the "old railway" buff to see before partaking of a well-earned drink or meal at the pub. From the pub proceed across the car park and onwards along the top of the escarpment, soon reaching a small grassy bank, turning left here and making your way to the very edge of the escarpment. Here you will see a small area of brickwork and metal which is all that remains of the upper end platform and engine house foundations of the Dyke Steep-Grade Railway carrying passengers from Poynings, the village you can see just at the bottom of the hill, to the Dyke's summit. Passengers were hauled to the summit in open-sided cars driven by an oil engine in conjunction with a cable. The line was opened in 1897 but was put up for sale just three years later and finally closed in 1908, the tracks being removed by the end of the First World War. Looking immediately downhill from the brickwork you can see the straight course taken by the old line; it is almost too steep to walk, the gradient being between 1 in 1.5 and 1 in 2.9, and in any case it disappears into woodland near the foot of the hill. From the platform remains, return to the pub from which buses are available back to Brighton, or alternatively you could retrace your steps to Aldrington on foot - downhill all the way!

The end of the Aldrington-Devil's Dyke route at Dyke Farm.

WALK 7 - **BRIGHTON TO KEMP TOWN**

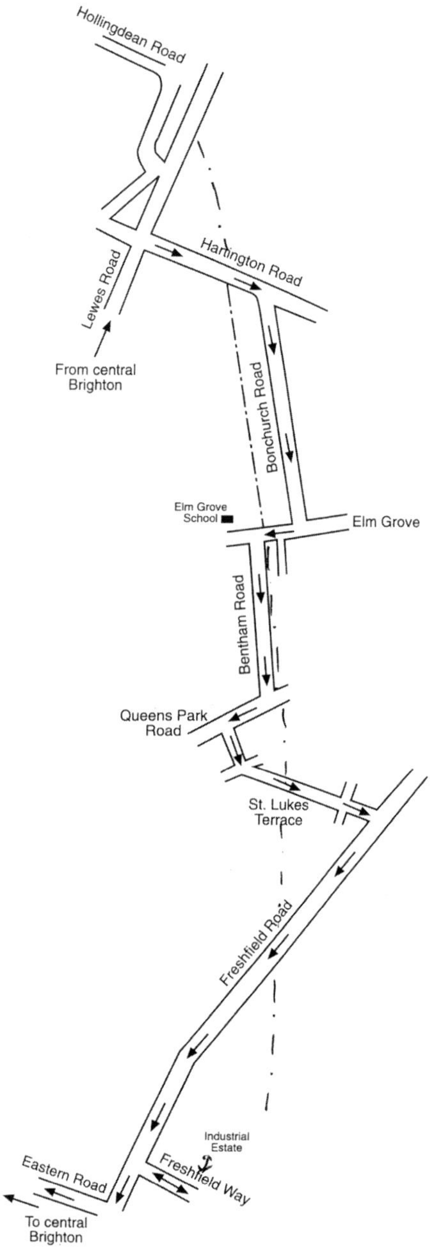

Hollingdean Road

Harrington Road

Lewes Road

From central Brighton

Bonchurch Road

Elm Grove School ■

Elm Grove

Bentham Road

Queens Park Road

St. Lukes Terrace

Freshfield Road

Industrial Estate

Eastern Road

Freshfield Way

To central Brighton

WALK 7 - BRIGHTON TO KEMP TOWN

Length:	1.5 miles.
Start:	Junction of Lewes Road and Hartington Road, Brighton.
Finish:	Freshfield Industrial Estate.
Public Transport:	Brighton is easily reachable by train from Portsmouth, Chichester, London, Lewes, Eastbourne and Hastings; excellent bus routes (BH) link the centre with the start and finish of the walk.
Refreshments:	Plenty of pubs, shops and cafes around the start of the walk; there are a couple of pubs on the walk itself but ample refreshment opportunities are just minutes away.
Conditions:	This isn't one of the most rewarding railway walks in Sussex and has curiosity value more than anything else. Very little trace of the old line remains, but the walk is at least extremely easy and shouldn't take more than an hour.

History

Kemp Town is now a bustling cosmopolitan area of Brighton with its own distinctive character; it was Thomas Kemp, who was responsible for developing the area in the 1820's, that gave the district its name. In May 1864 the go-ahead was given to the London, Brighton & South Coast Railway to build a line that linked central Brighton with Kemp Town, although it took five years for it to open. The railway followed the existing (and still surviving) Lewes line north-eastwards to just beyond London Road, only then branching off and heading seawards to reach Kemp Town, the terminus some way to the north-west of the area of Brighton of that name. Despite the shortness of the branch - about a mile - there were two intermediate halts, Lewes Road (opened in 1873)and Hartington Road (opened in 1906), two viaducts and a lengthy tunnel, and it was just beyond the tunnel that Kemp Town station was situated. An impressive 32 journeys were being made each day by 1906. However, following the First World War, the line went into decline, owing to competition from buses and trams which were able to ply much more direct courses between central Brighton and Kemp Town. It closed on 2nd January 1933, although the tunnel was used as an air-raid shelter during the Second World War, and in fact Kemp Town station stayed open until June 1971 for use as a goods vehicle depot. Sadly the viaducts have been demolished.

A section of the Brighton-Kemp Town line looking towards the long tunnel.

Walking the Line

Your walk starts at the junction of Lewes Road and Hartington Road to the north-east of central Brighton; it is a good 30-minute walk from the Brighton seafront via Old Steine, Grand Parade, Richmond Place and Lewes Road (A270). By continuing up Lewes Road beyond Hartington Road past a garage and Marks & Spencer foodstore/café on the left-hand side, you'll reach a junction with Hollingdean Road which goes off to the left. Looking along Hollingdean Road you'll see the bridge carrying the extant Brighton-Lewes line over the road, while the old line branched off it just to the left of the bridge and proceeded roughly parallel with Hollingdean Road on its south side (to your left as you look along the road), with Lewes Road halt situated on this stretch. Walking back to the junction with Hartington Road, you'll be passing the point where the old line crossed Lewes Road; its course is now covered by the big Sainsbury's just beyond the garage to the right, and there are no traces of it at all on either side of Lewes Road. Bear left into Hartington Road and follow the right-hand pavement, soon passing a prominent block of brick-built flats (which is on the right) beyond which is a signed entrance to William Clarke Park, also to your right. Take this entrance, climbing up onto the crest of the bank, and you will find yourself on the course of the old line, by the site of Hartington Road halt. From here, you can follow a strip of grass for a few hundred yards, this being the only piece of the old line that you can walk. Directly ahead of you is the boarded-up northern mouth of the tunnel, but the playground of Elm Grove County Primary School makes further progress towards the tunnel impossible, so you are forced to retrace your steps back to Hartington Road. Pausing at the crest of the bank, looking just west of north, you may be able to see the existing

Brighton-Lewes line in the middle distance and using the section of old line you have just followed as a marker you can see roughly the course that old line would have followed to link with the still existing line.

There is no access through the tunnel. Having returned to Hartington Road turn right then right again into Bonchurch Road, and at the end turn right into Elm Grove, getting a good view of the small strip of existing line you have just walked. It was at this point that the line entered the tunnel. Take the second left turn into Bentham Road then turn right at the T-junction into Queen's Park Road, and join it briefly before taking the second left turn into Queen's Park Terrace, just beyond St Luke's church. Follow this to the junction with Freshfield Road, turning right to follow this road, and soon you find yourself looking down on the Freshfield Industrial Estate to your left; passing the estate, you turn left into Freshfield Way and left again into Stevenson Road to gain access to the estate itself. Beyond you can see the steep cliffs from which the old line emerged. If you walk up to the top right (north-eastern) corner of Stevenson Road you'll be able to see the tunnel mouth although there's no chance of your being able to walk

all the way up to it. Walk back down to Freshfield Way, cross straight over it, and proceed through a car park area with a bingo hall to your right, the car park built on the site of the old Kemp Town station, and the terminus of the old line. To reach Kemp Town itself, and access the centre of Brighton, go forward to arrive almost immediately at Eastern Road and turn right, then turn first left into Upper Bedford Street. Follow this street to the junction of Bristol Road (to your left) with Upper St James's Street (to your right); to reach the centre of Brighton from Upper Bedford Street, turn right into Upper St James's Street and continue along St James's Street to arrive back at the Old Steine.

Part of the short walkable section of the Brighton-Kemp Town line looking back.

WALK 8 - LEWES TO UCKFIELD

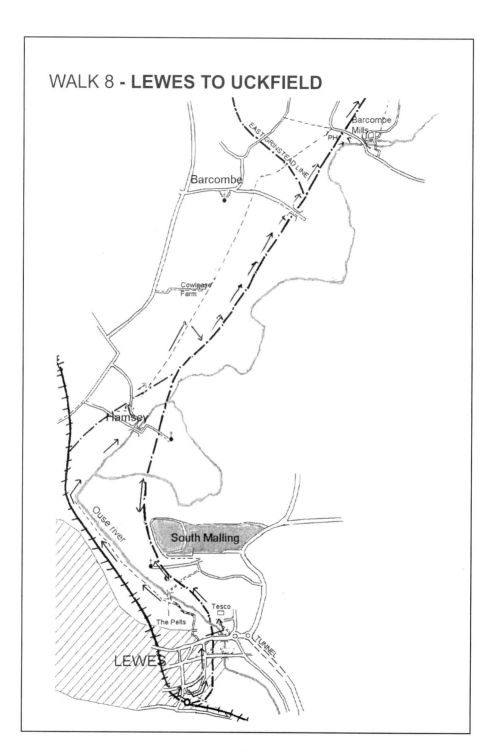

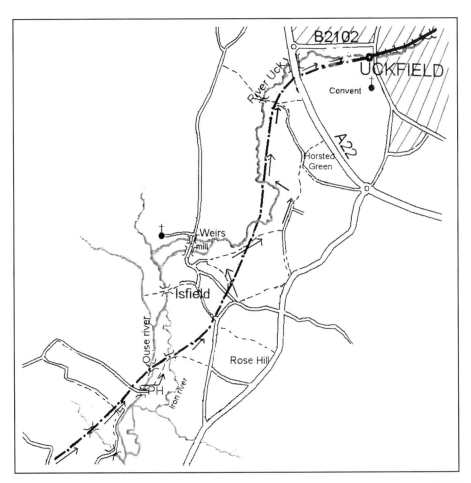

The Lewes-Uckfield line crossing of the Ouse near the popular Anchor pub at Barcombe.

WALK 8 - LEWES TO UCKFIELD

Length:	12 miles.
Start:	Lewes station.
Finish:	Uckfield station.
Public Transport:	Regular trains serving Lewes on the London Victoria-Hastings and Brighton-Seaford/Hastings routes; regular buses (BH) serving Uckfield on the Tunbridge Wells-Brighton route; regular trains from Uckfield to Oxted and London Victoria.
Refreshments:	Lewes (P,C,S); Barcombe (P); Isfield (P,C - occasional); Uckfield (P,C,S)
Conditions:	This is a tremendous walk, with several good sections of old line available for walking and very little road walking indeed. The scenery is delightful throughout. However, there are two caveats. Much of the walking is on private land with only one fairly short section of old line actually a public right of way, although it has to be said that many of the private sections are fairly easy to access. There is also a potential problem between Hamsey and Culver Farm in summer, where growing crops may make it difficult, if not impossible, to follow the described route. I would suggest you do this walk outside the late spring and summer months, but if you decide to take a chance, you should be prepared to turn back and follow the diversion suggested. It is imperative that you do not damage crops.

History

The London, Brighton & South Coast Railway (LBSCR) had arrived at Lewes, the county town of East Sussex, in the mid-1840's, and as early as 1844 there were suggestions for a link between Lewes and Uckfield, then an important agricultural centre. The Lewes & Uckfield Railway Company was established and, with the support of the LBSCR, opened the branch line from Lewes to Uckfield in 1858, services commencing on 11th October of that year. Ownership of the line was to pass to LBSCR during the following year. The branch line ran through flat countryside in the valleys of the Ouse and its tributary, the Uck, and there were no significant centres of population between the two towns.

For the first ten years it initially followed the line for Wivelsfield and Haywards Heath, heading north-westwards, before branching off at Uckfield Junction a short distance out of Lewes and then striking out north-eastwards. That was to change in 1868 (see below). The flatness of the terrain meant that no tunnels were necessary but there were a large number of crossings - more than sixteen - and several bridges were required, mostly under the line, including crossings of the Ouse. Just beyond Barcombe Mills two bridges in quick succession were needed to take the line across the two channels into which the Ouse divided at this point, one being known as the River Ouse Bridge, and the other known as Iron Bridge; much of the line was in fact barely above the river level, and flooding occurred from time to time. There were just two intermediate stations, serving relatively small villages. The first station on the line out of Lewes towards Uckfield was Barcombe Mills which was extremely popular with anglers, and during the 1920's upwards of a thousand train tickets were collected at Barcombe Mills from anglers on Bank Holidays. The second station was Isfield, virtually identical in construction to the one at Barcombe Mills: during the First World War Isfield saw considerable deliveries of milk churns, and the station was also an unloading point for prisoners of war who were doing forestry work in the area.

Ten years after the line opened, and nine years after the LBSCR takeover, there were two important events in the history of the line in quick succession. On 3rd August 1868 a line linking Uckfield with Tunbridge Wells came into being, allowing direct trains between Brighton and Tunbridge Wells via Falmer, Lewes, Uckfield, Crowborough and Eridge, and indeed it became theoretically possible to travel from London to Brighton using the Lewes-Uckfield section. Then on 1st October of the same year a new stretch of line was opened between Lewes and Hamsey, a short way east of Uckfield Junction, heading eastwards out of Lewes station and then proceeding more directly towards Barcombe Mills past Hamsey church. Not only did this allow a faster more direct journey, but it meant that trains that had started their journey from Brighton did not have to reverse back out of Lewes to continue towards Uckfield. This new section of line was shared with another branch line which left the Uckfield line at Culver Junction, just before Barcombe Mills, and proceeded northwards to East Grinstead via Sheffield Park and Horsted Keynes, these two stations well known as the original termini of the Bluebell Railway. The Lewes-East Grinstead line is described elsewhere in this book.

In 1869 there were six weekday trains going from Lewes to Uckfield and on to Tunbridge Wells (two on Sundays), while an 1890 timetable shows weekday trains leaving Lewes for Uckfield at 7.32am, 8.32am, 9.55am, 12.18pm, 2.05pm, 4.53pm, 6.02pm, 6.21pm, 7.38pm and 9.32pm, with many although not all of these trains going on to Tunbridge Wells. In 1912 some ten weekday trains were still plying the Lewes to Uckfield line each way; the first train of the day left Tunbridge Wells at 7am, arriving at Uckfield at 7.43am, Isfield at 7.49am, Barcombe Mills at 7.56am and Lewes at 8.05am. During the late 1930's daily through trains ran between Brighton and Chatham and also between Brighton and Reading, using the Uckfield line in each case.

The Lewes-Uckfield line was to be a victim of the Beeching axe in the 1960's, and following a steady reduction in the number of services, the last train ran on 23rd February 1969. However the line north of Uckfield was spared, leaving Uckfield effectively as a terminus. Ironically it is the station buildings of Barcombe Mills and Isfield that survive today, whilst Uckfield, which still boasts a railway service northwards towards Crowborough and Eridge, lost its original station comparatively recently and a brand new building has been constructed. In recent years there has been considerable pressure for the Lewes-Uckfield line to be reinstated, allowing for a link between the Victoria-Uckfield line and the network of routes that go out of Lewes towards Eastbourne, Hastings, Seaford, Brighton and Haywards Heath. So far attempts at reinstatement have not met with success; considerable sums would in any event have to be spent on restoring the river crossings, and the construction of a very large industrial estate on the course of the old line just south-west of Uckfield station has covered all trace of the old line and would seem to have frustrated any possibility of a through rail link. However, one part of the old line has survived. Following the purchase of Isfield station by the Milham family in 1983, that station was restored and the track nearby was relaid to allow trains to ply a small section of the old line to the north-east of the village; this small section became known as the Lavender Line, not because of the surrounding vegetation but after the coal merchants A.E. Lavender who used to operate from the station yard. Since then a Lavender Line preservation society has been established and it is possible to enjoy journeys from Isfield along this section of line on coaches hauled by old steam locomotives.

Walking The Line

The first section of route, although it skirts the centre of Lewes, follows the portion of line out of Lewes that opened in 1868 (hereafter the 1868 alignment). Leave Lewes station by the north (car park) exit beyond platform 1 and walk through the car park to exit it; beyond, bear right onto a narrow road which borders the car park (Pinwell Road), then shortly fork right along a footpath running roughly parallel with the existing line. You arrive at a footbridge over the railway, but just before it you fork left onto a path which can be quite muddy and enters an area quite dense with vegetation and with a semi-rural feel. In a few yards, fork left again and climb up onto an embankment, now for the first time on the 1868 alignment, and walking on it briefly before descending again, following the path to its end on the corner of Court Road. Go straight over the road crossing here into Court Road, and follow it to a T-junction, turning left and arriving at a junction with Friars Walk. Turn right into Friars Walk and follow it, continuing on into Eastgate Street past Waitrose - the old line followed a parallel course to your right throughout this section, but there's no trace of it now - then beyond Waitrose swing right onto Phoenix Causeway. Cross the road and continue along Phoenix Causeway over the Ouse, but pause before the crossing; a small fragment of railway embankment, covered with vegetation, still exists just to the left here, and, looking north-east across the river to the Tesco superstore, you are in fact viewing the point of the river where a bridge carried the old line over the water to the area now occupied by the store.

Immediately after crossing the river, turn left to follow the riverside path along the east bank, and having passed the Tesco store you will see a large area of green ahead of you. Follow this area of green north-westwards, keeping parallel with the river - this is the course of the old line - and aim for a raised green embankment a little to the right of the riverside path. Now (1) you have a choice. If you want to press on towards Uckfield, veer back towards the riverside path and walk on to the footbridge a little beyond the embankment. However, there's the option of detouring onto the embankment and joining the course of the newer realigned route between Lewes and Hamsey, being able to follow its course for what is a delightful walk of just over half a mile. You will pass under two bridges, and will emerge from the cuttings to enjoy a lovely green path

The Lewes-Uckfield line near Barcombe.

in open countryside with great views ahead of you, including Hamsey church, delightfully positioned on the hilltop. Unfortunately you reach a dead end, the Ouse now directly in front of you with no way across, and although you can follow the course of the old line beyond the river with your eyes, you will have to retrace your steps all the way back to (1) above, and now turn hard right to arrive at the footbridge which you use to cross over the Ouse. Immediately after crossing the footbridge, turn right onto a riverside path that keeps the river to the right and the railway across fields to the left. You proceed north-westwards but in just under a mile from the bridge, the river, and riverside path, swings north-eastwards. Looking north-westwards at this point, you can identify where the old line left the still extant main line during the first ten years

of its life. Shortly the river divides, your path continuing along the left bank of a narrow cut of the Ouse, and by Hamsey Place you reach a metalled road, Ivors Lane (2).
There's a chance of another detour here to view further parts of the 1868 alignment. If you want to miss it, turn left into Ivors Lane, but if you'd like to take it, turn right here and immediately cross a bridge over the cut of the Ouse, then swing sharp left and almost immediately sharp right, walking up the road towards Hamsey church. Very soon you'll reach the parapet of an overbridge crossing of the old line, and just before the bridge there's a gate on the right and a sign indicating CHURCH PARKING. You could go through or over this gate (when the gate is locked, there's no right of way beyond it, so please see my introductory notes) and join the obvious course of the old line as far as the remains of the bridge crossing of the Ouse. It's a delightful spot and you'll feel frustrated that the demolition of the bridge has broken the continuity. Now return to the road and turn left to retrace your steps back towards the crossing of the cut of the Ouse, but before the first bend look right to observe the course of the old line along a grassy embankment, soon to cross the cut of the Ouse a little further upstream. Because its course is so clear, and the way ahead is blocked by the cut, there's no point in trying to access it, so return to the cut the way you came, cross it and now bear right along the road. As it bends left, there's a gate (3) straight ahead beyond which is a path beside the cut, shortly leading to the old line's crossing of the cut, easily identifiable by the remains of the bridge. You could bear left, scramble up onto the old line here and follow it until you reach a junction with the old alignment, but your progress is then halted by barbed wire so you'll need to retrace your steps to the gate marked (3) above. I should emphasize that this gate has a notice stating the path beyond it is private and at the time of writing bulls are grazed in the adjacent field so you may decide to give it a miss, but if you're thinking of walking it, you must refer to my introductory notes. Whether you risk it or not, you now need to walk the short distance back to the bridge over the cut to reach point (2) above, and turn right to follow Ivors Lane.
Whether you took the detour or not, follow Ivors Lane briefly, heading north-westwards, and very soon you'll see the course of the 1858 alignment coming in from the left. If you want to detour back to have a look at it, turn left into the field on the near side of it, and follow the right-hand field edge; soon you'll be able to climb up onto the course of the 1858 alignment and follow it almost to where it left the extant Lewes-London line. Retrace your steps to Ivors Lane but this time cross straight over onto a signed path. Follow this path, which runs parallel with and immediately adjacent to the course of the 1858 alignment, then squeezes past the garden of a private house to arrive at another metalled road. Across the road, the old line can clearly be identified leading away in a north-easterly direction towards Barcombe Mills (the 1868 alignment meeting up with the 1858 alignment a little beyond this point) but unfortunately access is obstructed by a barbed wire-topped gate. You are forced to turn left and follow the metalled road briefly, soon arriving at a signed footpath leading off to the right, which you take; this path is well-defined and as it is set slightly above the course of the old

line, you get an excellent view to the course of the old line to your right as you walk. You follow a clear track, able at least to follow the course of the old line with your eyes, and go forward into an open field. Walk across to the far end of the field and, with the buildings of Cowlease Farm in sight, you reach a ditch coming in from the right, marked by a small flinty wall; turn right here, away from the public footpath, and follow the right bank of the ditch to arrive back at the course of the old line (4). It may be possible to backtrack but that will depend on what's being grown in the field and in any case at the end of the field further progress back to Hamsey is obstructed by a fence. So whether you've backtracked or not, now turn resolutely north-eastwards to follow the old line, which can, subject to two important caveats highlighted below, be followed now almost all the way to the old Barcombe Mills station. To begin with, all is well as you proceed initially on a clear track, but after just a couple of hundred yards or so you reach a field (5).

In winter, there should be no difficulty in going straight over it, aiming for a gate (6) beyond which the course of the old line is obvious, although as none of this, including the walk over the field, is on designated rights of way, you should refer to my introductory notes. You pass what is one of very few overbridges on the old line at Culver Farm, and shortly afterwards reach Culver Junction, the point where the East Grinstead branch left the Uckfield branch, easily identified by the obvious green embankment curving gracefully away to the left. If you are following the old line towards East Grinstead, you now need to refer on to the Lewes-East Grinstead chapter of this book. However, if you're proceeding towards Uckfield you can continue very pleasantly along the well-defined course of the old line, until you reach a gate obstructing further progress; beyond the gate are the old station buildings and grounds of Barcombe Mills. Retrace your steps a hundred yards or so, looking out carefully for and crossing a stile on the left, then having crossed the stile, bear left and walk through the meadows close by the left bank of the Ouse, aiming just to the left of the road bridge crossing where there's a gate. Pass through the gate and bear left onto the road, soon reaching Barcombe Mills station.

However, the walking in the above paragraph will become problematic if crops are being grown in the field referred to at (5) above. Moreover, the gate by the road bridge crossing referred to in the final two sentences of the above paragraph is likely to be locked. There MAY be sufficient room for you to bear right and follow the right-hand field edge round to the gate at (6) above taking great care not to damage any crops, but you really should seek permission before doing this; if proceeding on to Uckfield, you MAY be prepared to surmount the locked gate referred to at the end of the above paragraph. If you are unable to get round the field edge without damage to crops, OR you are going on to Uckfield and are unwilling to surmount the gate, you'll need to retrace your steps all the way back to (4) above, then bear right to follow the left-hand side of the ditch and arrive back at the small flinty wall where you rejoin the public footpath. Turn right now to follow this footpath, actually the Ouse Valley Way, soon passing Cowlease Farm. Beyond Cowlease Farm there are two footbridge crossings in close succession, and there's a fork left to Barcombe church; ignore this fork and go forward to arrive at a broad track linking Barcombe with Culver Farm. Cross straight over on a well-defined albeit narrow path which after skirting some private housing turns sharply right and descends gently across a field to a footbridge. Just a short way ahead of you now is the course of the old line branching off to East Grinstead: if you're planning to follow this, you can simply carry straight on, soon arriving at and crossing the course of that line, using the description in the Lewes-East Grinstead chapter. However if you're wanting to go on to Uckfield, you should bear right at the footbridge to follow the left-hand field edge round to the side of the embankment of the old East Grinstead branch, and then walk beside it along the field edge to arrive beside Culver Junction where the Uckfield and East Grinstead lines parted. You can access the Uckfield line here. Once on the old line, you could turn right to detour back to the gate referred to at (6) above, following the old line, and returning to Culver Junction the same way but whether you've detoured or not, you now simply follow the instructions given above to walk from Culver Junction via the old line to Barcombe Mills station.

Some years ago, the old station served as a café, but at the time of writing it was very definitely private and inaccessible to walkers. The good news, however, is that by turning right immediately opposite the station you can now join the old line for the next mile, heading north-eastwards; the going is very straightforward through pleasant unspoilt countryside. It is a shame when you reach Anchor Lane and discover the way ahead is blocked off, so turn right onto Anchor Lane and very shortly reach the deservedly popular Anchor Inn with its delightful garden that backs onto the Ouse. Beyond the Anchor, use the footbridge to cross the river, then bear left and follow its right bank,

Isfield station, headquarters of the Lavender Line using part of the Lewes-Uckfield line.

soon reaching the course of the old line again. It is possible to climb up onto the line (attacking it from the far side) and follow it north-eastwards; this is not a designated right of way but there is no difficulty of access, and it's very pleasant walking. In three quarters of a mile or so, you pass the Boathouse farm buildings which are to your right, and a little beyond the buildings you reach a dead end. You need to access Lewes Road which is beyond the farm to the right, and it may be possible to do this simply by backtracking a few yards, turning left and walking through the farm outbuildings to the road. If that's not possible you'll need to backtrack along the old line, keeping an eye open for a very obvious pond about a quarter of a mile back on your left; bear left off the old line round to the south tip of the pond, then bear very briefly right to pick up a path which now runs just south of east to arrive at Lewes Road. However you've reached Lewes Road, turn left onto it and follow it northwards to Isfield and its beautifully preserved station. Beyond the station, you continue along Horsted Lane - to the right of the station complex - but if time allows, you should certainly explore the station, with its wonderful reminders of when through trains between Lewes and Uckfield did exist, and travel on one of the steam trains that ply the Lavender Line, that very small stretch of preserved line that runs north-eastwards from here. Refreshments are available at the nearby pub. Incidentally, do not trespass onto the preserved line; you may be committing an offence, and in any case there's no way forward at the other end.

You proceed briefly along Horsted Lane, which bends right and then right again; at the second bend turn hard left onto a signed path (there are two paths here; you need the one going hard left) and head north-westwards to soon arrive at and cross over the preserved line. With the single track in the cutting, railway paraphernalia in view and the Downs in the background, there's a slight feel of Thomas the Tank Engine about it all! Beyond the crossing your path veers right to run all too briefly parallel with the line but almost at once goes off left, north-westwards, and then swings left again, going downhill towards the buildings of Tile Barn Farm. You pass a barn which is to your right, and beyond the barn you reach a path junction where you turn right; you cross a small green area between the farm buildings, going gently downhill, and soon reach another path junction. Go straight ahead along a clearer path which leaves the farm buildings and descends to arrive at the river Uck, and looking to the right from here, across the river, it is possible to view the Lavender Line. You bear right to follow the right (south) bank of the Uck briefly, then use a footbridge to cross over the river and follow the left bank, ignoring a path going off to the left. Keeping to the path and heading north-eastwards, you temporarily lose the river at a meander round a small patch of woodland but are soon reunited with it again and now swing in an easterly direction. You shortly meet the old line, just north of the point where the preserved section ends, although the bridge conveying the continuation of the line over the Uck, and over your path, is now effectively a shell. To make progress towards Uckfield from here you need to carry straight on eastwards, aiming for a footbridge over the Uck (7), but it's possible to veer left immediately beyond the bridge, follow the left-hand field edge briefly and here (8) join the old line which can be followed for a little over a quarter of a mile. Unfortunately you reach a dead end, in the form of another Uck crossing, with no way over it, so you must return to (8) above and then walk diagonally across the field to reach the footbridge over the Uck at (7) above.

Beyond the footbridge, continue along the path which skirts the southern edge of an area of woodland, and drops to arrive at a narrow metalled road. Turn left to follow it shortly, soon arriving at a flood height indicator, then immediately beyond the indicator turn left onto a green track which proceeds delightfully back to reach the right bank of the Uck. The track peters out at a field, and you simply follow the field edge, passing a weir and arriving back at the course of the old line just across the river from the dead end referred to in the final sentence of the paragraph above. Although none of it is a designated right of way, it is actually possible to follow the old line from here all the way to the A22 crossing on the outskirts of Uckfield. The scenery through the trees is delightful; there are no obstructions, and it's super walking. You pass the buildings of Owlsbury Farm which are just to your right, and beyond the farm the going gets rougher and the sound of traffic on the very busy A22 Uckfield by-pass becomes more intrusive. Drop down off the embankment, and scramble up to arrive at the A22 which you cross straight over with extreme care. Pass into a car park adjoining business premises which are to your left, and walk through the car park, veering left at the end and then right to enter Brambleside, a road through the Horsted Square industrial estate, the course of the old line parallel with you to the right. Note, however, that you may not be able to enter Brambleside from the car park - it is signed as private and the access gates may be locked - and if so you'll need to backtrack to the A22, turn right and follow it (a pretty hateful walk, I have to say) to the B2102 roundabout junction, turn right onto the B2102 and then first right into Brookside which you follow over the river Uck to a T-junction with Brambleside at the very end.

Now follow Brambleside towards Uckfield (just north of east), the course of the old line just to your right. The road peters out but you're able to continue on along a metalled path which rises and goes forward to a grassy area, with new housing development to your right. On reaching the grassy area, bear right and follow the right-hand edge of the grass, veering round and now seeing the old line in a cutting to the right. Make your way carefully down the bank - it's not too steep! - and join the old line which you can now follow much of the rest of the way to Uckfield, although this isn't a designated right of way and progress may be made more difficult by flooded sections or pieces of debris. At length you arrive at a metalled fence beyond which progress appears to be impossible. However just short of the fence you can veer to the left and, taking enormous care, follow a crude path round the left-hand edge of the fence (if in doubt, don't attempt it) and by following this path you'll find yourself walking along or beside pieces of old track from when the line still existed, and in due course you arrive at the old Uckfield station platform. Looking ahead, you can see the new station and the start/finish of the extant London line. However there's no way through, so you'll need to backtrack to the west side of the metalled fence you had to negotiate a few moments ago. Whether you've made this little detour or not, retrace your steps from the metalled fence and shortly turn hard left (south-eastwards) to follow a rough path leaving the old line and climbing quite steeply. Soon, however, you reach a T-junction with a much clearer path. Turn left here and follow the path which climbs through pleasant woodland and arrives at a crossroads of paths with housing to the left, bearing left at this crossroads and soon arriving at a gate which gives access to Bridge Farm Road. Bear left to follow this road down to Uckfield High Street; by turning left into the High Street you'll almost immediately reach the new station which is to the right, and beyond is the town itself which has all the amenities a tired walker could wish for, To access buses to Lewes, turn left onto the B2102 Bell Lane and you'll almost immediately see the bus station on your left.

The present-day Uckfield station viewed from the northern end of the old line coming up from Lewes.

WALK 9 - LEWES TO EAST GRINSTEAD / HAYWARDS HEATH TO HORSTED KEYNES

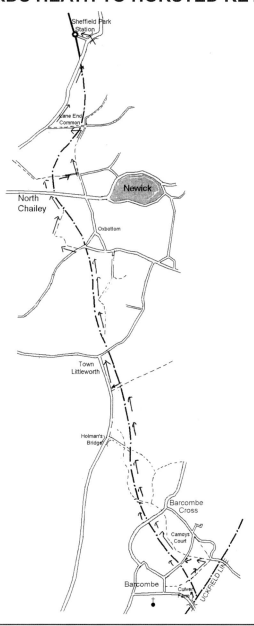

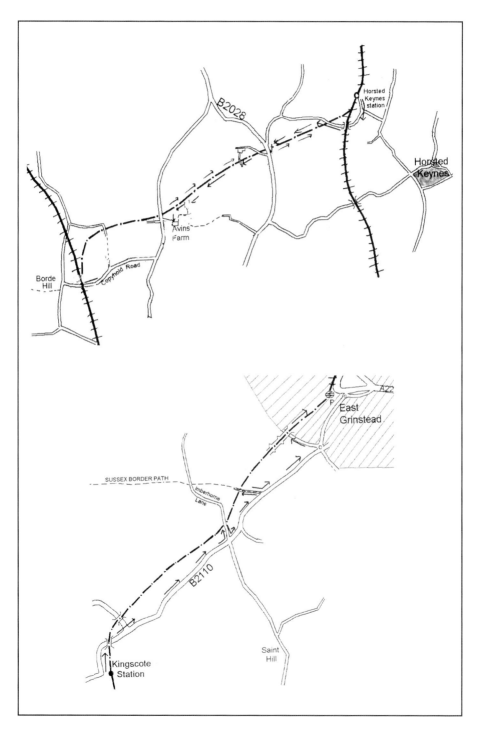

WALK 9 - LEWES TO EAST GRINSTEAD / HAYWARDS HEATH TO HORSTED KEYNES

Length:	approximately 11 miles of walking in total.
Start:	Lewes station.
Finish:	Horsted Keynes (Bluebell Railway) station. However, public transport links from here are infrequent, and in practice you'll want to ride the Bluebell Railway on to Kingscote or, when the Bluebell Railway extension is complete, East Grinstead. Please study the text below carefully.
Public Transport:	Regular trains to Lewes from London Victoria, Brighton, Seaford, Eastbourne and Hastings; regular buses (CL) serving North Chailey and Newick on the Haywards Heath-Uckfield route; regular trains on the Bluebell Railway from Sheffield Park to Horsted Keynes and Kingscote with bus connections to East Grinstead; regular trains from East Grinstead to East Croydon and London Victoria; regular buses (MB) serving East Grinstead on the Tunbridge Wells-Three Bridges-Crawley route.
Refreshments:	Lewes (P,C,S); Barcombe Cross (P,S); Newick (slightly off route) (P,S); Sheffield Park (P,C); Horsted Keynes (P,C); East Grinstead (P,C,S).
Conditions:	Although not a single stretch of old line covered in this chapter has been turned into a designated right of way, most of it is followable, albeit some scrambling is necessary in places. The scenery is very attractive and it is well worth the effort. The whole walk will require a day to accomplish, and to gain maximum enjoyment from it, you really need to do it on a day when the Bluebell Railway is running, as a ride on the Bluebell Railway is an integral part of this journey. It is therefore assumed, for the purpose of what follows, that the Bluebell Railway is running; opening days - and there are plenty - are easily found on their website or in tourist information offices. Check the times carefully and plan your itinerary to avoid getting to the Bluebell Railway after services have finished for the day!

History

Whilst the line between Lewes and Uckfield opened in 1858, with the "short cut" route from Lewes to Hamsey opening ten years later (see walk 8 above), it was not until 1877 that statutory approval was given to construct the line that was to provide a link between Lewes and East Grinstead, using part of the Lewes to Uckfield route. A company known as the Lewes & East Grinstead Railway Company, formed in 1875, had masterminded the plans for the new route, and once Royal assent was given, the London, Brighton & South Coast Railway (LBSCR) took it over and oversaw the construction of the line which opened in August 1882. Meanwhile, in July 1880, the LBSCR obtained permission to open a link line between Horsted Keynes, on the new Lewes to East Grinstead line, and Haywards Heath on the main London to Brighton line. This opened in 1883.

The Lewes to East Grinstead line followed the course of the Lewes to Uckfield line to not far short of Barcombe station, branching off at Culver Junction just beyond Culver Farm. Effectively a second station for Barcombe was opened a mile or so north of Culver Junction on the East Grinstead line; it was known as New Barcombe but then changed to Barcombe while Barcombe station on the Uckfield line became Barcombe Mills! A pleasant cross-country journey through a very sparsely-populated area brought the line to its next halt, Newick & Chailey, and thence to Fletching & Sheffield Park although the Fletching part was dropped just a year after opening. Beyond Sheffield Park, as Bluebell Railway enthusiasts will know, came Horsted Keynes, which was a remarkable station; it was the junction for trains to and from Haywards Heath, and was well-

A lovely sunlit view back to the start of the East Grinstead branch at Culver Junction.

Barcombe station on the Lewes-East Grinstead line.

appointed and sizeable with a sturdy red-brick station building and platforms that benefited from canopies. Yet save for the small nearby village of the same name, there was no apparent source of passenger traffic. Beyond Horsted Keynes was West Hoathly, these two stations being separated by the 731-yard West Hoathly Tunnel; after West Hoathly the line descended to Kingscote, and just over a mile beyond that, East Grinstead was reached. Immediately before East Grinstead there was constructed, and remains, what is arguably the most impressive surviving feature of the old line, the ten-arch red-brick Imberhorne Viaduct, and even today, surrounded by modern housing, this magnificent feat of engineering dominates the landscape. There was only one station on the link line to Haywards Heath from Horsted Keynes, namely Ardingly, and the station building still survives today. Incidentally this branch was electrified in July 1935 but the intervention of the Second World War caused electrification of the line to East Grinstead to be put on hold; as it was, steam trains continued to ply the East Grinstead line right up until closure.

The Lewes to East Grinstead line soon became extremely popular. By the beginning of the 20th century some twenty trains worked the line each day, carrying not only passengers but freight which included fruit, corn and milk. However traffic began to decline as the 20th century progressed, and it was decided to close the Lewes to East Grinstead line on 17th June 1955. The closure provoked a good deal of protest, and much to British Railways' embarrassment it was found by one Miss Bessemer of Chailey that closure could only be brought about by Parliamentary authority, pursuant to an Act of 1878, and not by the unilateral say-so of the railway company. The line therefore re-opened in 1956. During the brief period of its revival it was known as the "sulky service," with trains run during the middle of the day when they would have been of little use to anybody, and not stopping at certain stations that were not mentioned in the Act. This farcical situation could not continue indefinitely, and in due course a fresh Act of Parliament enabled the line to close legally in March 1958 although the line north of Horsted Keynes remained open on a "care and maintenance" basis for two more years. However, in 1960 a society for the preservation of the railway was formed, and the result was one of the best-loved preserved railways in the country. Known as the Bluebell Railway, it initially ran trains between Sheffield Park and Horsted Keynes but subsequently was able to extend to Kingscote; at the time of writing an extension to East Grinstead, linking with the main rail network, is in preparation and by the time you read this, it may be up and running. The link between Horsted Keynes and Haywards Heath survived until October 1963 when the section from Horsted Keynes to Ardingly closed altogether. However the section from Ardingly, to link with the main line just north of Haywards Heath, did remain open for goods traffic and is in fact still in use today.

Walking The Line

This walk is really in two or three parts. The first, and by far the longest, goes from Lewes, where the old line started, to Sheffield Park, where the Bluebell Railway takes over; the second starts at Horsted Keynes, further up the Bluebell Railway, and proceeds along the old Haywards Heath branch as far as Ardingly; the third runs from Kingscote, further still up the Bluebell Railway, to East Grinstead, but this will be redundant once the hoped-for extension of the Bluebell Railway to East Grinstead takes place.

The section of the old line between Lewes and Culver Junction, just beyond Hamsey, follows exactly the course of the old Lewes to Uckfield line, and is fully described in the chapter devoted to that line. The description that follows below begins at the point just beyond the overbridge at Culver Farm, where the green embankment is seen departing gracefully away from the Uckfield line going off to the left. This is the first part of the East Grinstead branch. Disappointingly you can't access it at this point, but on the Culver Farm side of the embankment you can access the adjacent field and follow the right-hand field edge round, tantalisingly separated from the embankment by a fence. Having worked your way round, veering slightly away from the embankment in fact, you meet and turn right onto the signed Ouse Valley Way footpath, a splendid route linking Lower Beeding with Newhaven. (NOTE - if because of growing crops you've been forced to divert away from the course of the Uckfield line, you'll actually have approached this point using the Ouse Valley Way anyway!) Now follow the Ouse Valley Way as signed and you'll soon find yourself crossing a stile and arriving on the embankment bearing the old line. It is possible to walk back from here down the embankment towards Culver Junction - and briefly the other way, too - and get a taste of the old line for the first time. However, you can't progress meaningfully in either direction so retrace your steps, leave the embankment by a stile opposite to that you used to join it, and continue on along the clear path. Proceeding along it, away from the old line, you begin to climb towards a road, and as you climb you reach a fence and stile; don't go over the stile but bear left, keeping the fence to your right, and you reach another stile in the fence, turning left here and now following a clear path through the field which drops down to a road.

Turn left to follow the road, and very soon arrive at a bridge over the old line. Immediately beyond the bridge you can turn right and drop down the bank onto the old line, turning left to join a path which now proceeds very pleasantly and easily on towards the next village, Barcombe Cross. Unfortunately the going does become rougher, the vegetation rather than any man-made obstacles impeding progress; I advise you to try and use the left edge of the course of the old line to negotiate them. Shortly the woodland to the left gives way to a field, and progress along this field edge is barred by a fence, but it is then possible to get back onto the course of the old line and you can follow it without too much difficulty until you get within sight of an overbridge carrying the Barcombe Cross-Hamsey road. There's no way under the overbridge, so scramble up the bank to the right - it isn't that steep, so you shouldn't have a problem - and turn left to follow the left-hand field edge to a little gate at the top corner of the field. Pass through the gate and go forward to the road via the garden of the adjacent house. Don't worry - it is a right of way! The village of Barcombe Cross, with a pub and shop, is immediately to the right, but you need to bear left and follow the road over the bridge. Shortly beyond the bridge there's a signed road junction. Take the right fork here, then turn immediately right along a track signed Stepney Farm (see bracketed note at the end of this paragraph); when the track ends, go straight on across the field to the far end, then at the far end bear left and go forward along the right-hand field edge. Very soon, through the trees on the right, you will see the former Barcombe station building on the right-hand side, but you can't get any closer to it, as the old line in front of it and either side of it is inaccessible. Continue on along the right-hand field edge, immediately parallel with the course of the old line on the north side of the old station, keeping houses on the right. Beyond the houses, the field starts to rise, and a gap in the hedge to your right allows you to join the course of the old line; its course could not be clearer, as a line of electricity/telegraph wires has been built along it! (NOTE - The track signed Stepney Farm is gated; should it be locked, you may wish to retrace your steps along the road, walk into Barcombe Cross, bear left off the main street into Grange Road, going forward onto a footpath by a sports field then descending and veering left with the path to arrive at the course of the old line with the electricity/telegraph wires as described above.)

Some excellent walking along the course of the old line now follows. Interestingly, it isn't signed or marked on OS maps as a right of way, but there is no express or implied prohibition on access and the way is remarkably and beautifully clear. The wires and

Though not a public right of way, there is no difficulty gaining access to this section of the Lewes-East Grinstead line just north of Barcombe.

poles, if rather unsightly, at least provide an unerring guide to the course to be followed, and you can enjoy walking through some very attractive countryside. In a few hundred yards you pass a sewage works, and a couple of hundred yards or so beyond that are the remains of a bridge over a footpath (1); and not far beyond that you pass beneath a fine overbridge but, just as you're really getting into your stride, the ground rises and you find yourself at a crossing track; the way forward along the old line is blocked first by undergrowth and then a gate which can't realistically be surmounted. Accordingly turn left to follow the crossing track westwards - a sign warns you to keep off it, so you should seek permission first - then veer slightly right with the track, away from the house and grounds immediately in front of you, and go forward along the track to reach a road (2), turning right. If you prefer not to access the road using this route from the old line, it'll be necessary for you to retrace your steps to just short of the bridge over the footpath referred to at (1) above; turn left down the bank, then turn right at the bottom of the bank, turn right again to join the footpath and follow it under the bridge then continue along the path across the field to the road, turning right to follow the road to the point at (2) above. Whichever route you've opted for, walk along the road in a north or north-westerly direction, soon arriving at a T-junction with another road. Turn right at this junction and soon you'll arrive at the point (3) where the old line crossed this road, the embankment going off to the left clearly marking its course. It is theoretically possible to bear right here, scrambling up the bank and following the course of the old line back to within shouting distance of the crossing track where you had to leave it. But while the electricity wires clearly show the course of the old line, progress is messy and difficult with frequent obstructions in the form of trees and undergrowth, and it's probably not worth the effort unless time is on your side.

Continuing on, then, from the point at (3) above, bear left, just west of north, off the road along a signed footpath, Cockfield Lane, which initially runs parallel with and immediately to the right of the embankment bearing the course of the old line. However this path is destined to part company with the embankment. You now have a choice. The safer route is simply to continue along Cockfield Lane, going downhill to cross a

river, then, veering north-eastwards, rise to meet a metalled road and turn left to follow the road to a bridge over the old line (4). However, it is possible, with difficulty, to follow the old line to the point at (4) above, although you should be warned it is quite tough going in places. If you decide to give it a go, bear left off Cockfield Lane while it hugs the foot of the embankment, scramble up onto the embankment to join the course of the old line, and simply follow it. Progress is fitful, with trees and undergrowth frequently getting in the way, but do persevere; the cutting relents and the going becomes really very enjoyable indeed, with lovely countryside to be seen on both sides of the old line and no express or implied prohibitions on access. Progressing well on what is a clearly defined course of the old line, you leave the thicker woodland behind and find yourself walking on grass, with an impressive looking property not far ahead of you to your left, but your progress then appears to be obstructed by thick woodland. However if you bear left you will

A delightful wooded section of the Lewes-East Grinstead line south of Newick.

see there is a thin path which enters and threads a way through the trees, sticking to the course of the old line. The old line now goes forward into what is a very deep cutting; you need to take a path which skirts the left side of the cutting, rising through the trees so that you're above the cutting and looking down on the course of the old line. The path becomes indistinct and really gives out altogether, but you're joined by a fence which is to the left, and it is possible for you to continue through the trees to arrive at the metalled road and its crossing of the old line referred to at (4) above. Whichever route you've taken, you need to proceed briefly south-westwards along the metalled road away from the old line here. It is possible to cross over the road and follow a crude path parallel with the old line on the far side and descending steeply, getting a view to the overbridge crossing, but progress forward with the old line is impossible so return to the road and now follow it shortly south-westwards as stated above. Your road walk is short-lived, however, for very shortly you need to bear

The Lewes-East Grinstead line just a little south of Sheffield Park and the start of the Bluebell Railway.

right along a signed path. The path crosses a field and enters woodland, whereupon you immediately reach a crossroads of footpaths; turn right here onto a path which at once bends left and goes forward to some farm buildings which looked rather sorry for themselves at the time of writing. Turn right immediately in front of the buildings and follow the clear path downhill through the trees, keeping woods to the right and fields to the left. The path emerges from the wood but continues downhill along the right-hand field edge, and crosses a stile to enter further woodland; keep on along the very obvious path through the woods, particularly attractive in the spring with a profusion of bluebells hereabouts. The path, having followed a straight line for a few hundred yards, now veers from north-eastwards to north-westwards, being reunited with the old line which comes in from the right - you really haven't missed a lot of it. You now follow parallel with and immediately to the left of the old line, the course of which runs through the back gardens of the houses to your right. Keeping the course of the old line just to your right, including the site of the old Newick & Chailey station, go forward to arrive at the A272 on the edge of Newick; the old line passed under this road, but the cutting has been filled in and all traces of the line in the immediate vicinity have disappeared. Buses are available at North Chailey (along the A272 to the west) and Newick (along the A272 to the east) should you feel you've done enough for today or for whatever reason you will be unable to ride the Bluebell Railway.

Cross more or less straight over the A272 into the metalled cul-de-sac Coldharbour Lane, going downhill to its end. When you reach the end, bear right onto a path the signpost for which at the time of

The tunnel on the Horsted Keynes-Ardingly line which is open and provides an adventurous interlude on this walk.

writing was broken, but if you find yourself going past the field belonging to the adjacent stables, you've gone too far. Having joined this path, you follow it, keeping the field to your left, and shortly beyond it you see the embankment of the old line clearly going away to the left, although its course from the A272 to this point is a good deal less clear. It's theoretically possible to pass through a gate into the field immediately beyond the embankment to the left, and then use another gate in the field to access the embankment, but all too soon you reach fencing and you can go no further. So return to the path and now follow it eastwards from the embankment and adjacent gate, having to satisfy yourself with following the course of the old line with your eyes as it heads towards Sheffield Park. Soon you reach the buildings of Cox's Farm and immediately beyond them you reach a junction with a signed bridleway and you turn left to follow it. It proceeds very pleasantly indeed through the woods, with glimpses through the trees and across the fields to the course of the old line which gets closer to you with each step. Shortly you arrive at a road and turn left to arrive almost immediately at a bridge over the old line (5), which is in a deep cutting at this point.

Now you have a difficult decision which may depend on your physical fitness and preparations made in advance of your walk. It is possible - I put it no higher than that - to use a gap between the right-hand bridge parapet on the near side and the adjoining private house, scramble across rough grass and then make your way carefully down the steep embankment to join the old line; there are no manmade bars to progress, but you do need to take immense care with your descent. Even assuming you reach the bottom in one piece, the course of the track bed is not without its obstructions, including fallen trees and waterlogged areas. But if you persevere, you will emerge from the cutting and pass into a field - still on the course of the old line - with houses across the field to your left and a modest line of trees just to your right, forming a crude boundary with a further field beyond. I was challenged as I made my way across this field so do make sure you have permission from the owner to cross it; if you cross it without permission, neither my publisher nor I can accept responsibility for the consequences. Assuming all is well, you aim for the tree-shaded embankment ahead, dropping down to a driveway and then rising up to join the embankment and follow it. It's now very easy going, save for one gate which you'll need to negotiate, and in due course you drop down the embankment, which may prove awkward but no more than that, to arrive at the A275 at Sheffield Park. I must re-emphasize that none of this is designated as a right of way, so please refer to my introductory notes.

If you decide against attempting this section, there is a safe and not too lengthy detour. Continue over the bridge from point (5) above and then turn immediately right onto a track, straightaway then turning left onto a path that goes forward onto Lane End Common. The path initially runs more or less parallel with the road then, within sight of an information board and parking area, veers away to the right, losing height. It then veers round to the left, forming a reverse U shape; very soon after negotiating this reverse U (so you're effectively facing back up the incline), look out for and take a path going off to the right, with traffic on the A275 visible to your left through the trees. The path heads into woodland, seemingly away from the road, but you need to take the next left-hand path turning which brings you to the A275. Turn right now to follow the A275 for about half a mile to be reunited with the embankment of the old line coming in from the right.

The course of the old line on the far side of the A275 can't be followed, so keep walking along the left (west) side of the road until you shortly reach the signed turning to

Sheffield Park station. Take this, and make your way up the approach road to the station with its many amenities including pub, café and superbly stocked shop. You can stroll down to the south end of the station and look back towards the ground you've just covered, then after enjoying something to eat or drink, board your Bluebell Railway train to Horsted Keynes. It's certainly good to let the train take the strain after your often tough walk from Lewes, and you'll perhaps wish the preserved line could have been extended southwards!

Alighting from Horsted Keynes, take the main exit from the station and follow the station approach road to its end, then turn right at the T-junction to follow the road that soon passes underneath the Bluebell Railway. The road bends to the right and almost immediately beyond the bend you'll see, on both sides, the embankment of the old line that formed the branch between Horsted Keynes and Haywards Heath. Follow the road round to the left, the embankment to the left separated from you by fencing, then when shortly the fencing relents you can scramble up the embankment to join the course of the old line. You're now able to follow it almost all the way to Ardingly. Although only a small section of it is designated as a right of way, there are no manmade obstructions to access at all; things are quite squelchy underfoot as you get going, but, temporarily at least, the going gets firmer and the walking is very pleasant indeed. You then reach one of the real highlights of this walk, a tunnel under a road crossing, and you are able to walk through it. It is perfectly safe but do take care as it is quite dark in the middle of the tunnel and you may get wet from water dropping from the top of the tunnel to the ground below. As so many disused railway tunnels are boarded up, it is a great privilege and thrill to go through this one.

Beyond the tunnel, the going gets very much tougher, with extremely muddy conditions underfoot and a good deal of tree branches to negotiate; however, do persevere because things improve, with a reasonably clear path and pleasant surroundings. You're forced to drop down to the right in order to get past a collapsed bridge, but having crossed the track you climb some steps to return to the course of the old line and, for a time, you're on a right of way along the old line, enjoying what really is lovely walking in the shade of woodland. The right of way leaves the course of the line but you can keep going along the old trackbed until the path deteriorates, obstructions accumulate and your way is blocked just short of an overbridge, now just a short distance from Ardingly station. Retrace your steps for a hundred yards or so back from the overbridge, until you reach a gate leading into a field to the right, with the buildings of Avins Farm just across the field. Use the gate to enter the field, and follow the right-hand field edge round (you could detour at the top of the field to get onto the overbridge and observe the course of the old line going forward to Ardingly station) until, just before the farm buildings, you're able to turn right to exit the field and enter another. Bear left to follow the left-hand field edge, keeping the farm buildings to your left, crossing a stile and reaching the farm approach road. Turn right to follow the farm approach road to a junction with College Road, turn right onto this road and very shortly you will reach the former

Ardingly station building. Immediately before it, a road leads into the Hanson industrial estate and it is here that your walk along this branch has to end; beyond the estate the track is in situ all the way to the junction with the main London-Brighton railway line just north of Haywards Heath and as stated above, this section remains in use for goods traffic today.

Now you have a choice. You could retrace your steps down College Road and follow it all the way into Haywards Heath which is a good 2 miles away. However, for completeness, I recommend you make your way back to the old line the same way, and follow it back towards Horsted Keynes again; it will of course mean another trudge through the mud on the Ardingly side of the road tunnel, but it beats road walking! Once beyond the road tunnel on the Horsted Keynes side, you'll need to look out carefully for your exit, and I suggest that it's probably easiest to walk as far as you can go, until you reach the far end of the embankment within sight and sound of the Bluebell Railway, then backtrack a little and bear right, down the slope to arrive back at the road. Turn right to follow the road round to the right, between the two portions of embankment. There is a gate (6) in the fence to the left just beyond the embankment, and by surmounting that and negotiating the vegetation beyond, you could **(but see my qualification in bold immediately below)** then climb up on to the embankment and follow the course of the old line to its link with the Bluebell Railway at Horsted Keynes station. You soon find yourself walking alongside a section of actual line and passing some old rolling stock, in due course reaching one of the side platforms of the station. **However it must be emphasized that it is absolutely essential to seek permission to do this.** If permission is not forthcoming, you should return to Horsted Keynes station by the road beyond the gate at (6) above, passing under the Bluebell Railway and taking the next left turn.

Once back at Horsted Keynes station, you may well wish to avail yourself of refreshment and the chance to wander round what is an extraordinarily large station for such a remote spot, before joining the Bluebell Railway again. It is hoped that by the time you read this, the extension to East Grinstead will have been completed, in which case you can regard your day's labour to be at an end, and enjoy a splendid ride which includes the West Hoathly Tunnel and the Imberhorne Viaduct, ending at East Grinstead. However at the time of writing the Bluebell Railway goes only as far as the immaculately kept Kingscote station. You could walk from Kingscote to East Grinstead, but I should point out that although there are glimpses of the old line between these places, it is quite impossible to walk any of the old line itself and a lot of the walk is alongside a busy road with no pavement. So you may prefer to take one of the buses which connect from Kingscote station to East Grinstead.

If you do decide to walk it, leave Kingscote station by the front entrance, turn right onto the road and follow it under the old line (inaccessible from here), going forward to a T-junction with the B2110, turning right and following it; this is not a particularly pleasant walk, as the road is very busy and there is no pavement. Just over half a mile after joining the B2110 you reach a crossroads, and detouring left along Imberhorne Lane offers, very shortly, another opportunity to view the old line as it passes under the lane. At the time of writing the track had been relaid to the left (coming up from Kingscote) while to the right the trackbed was buried under what looked like a landfill site. Don't even think about trying to join the old line. Return to the B2110 and turn left to follow it on towards East Grinstead, initially uphill and then downhill; thankfully you do now have a pavement, but the surroundings are really no more congenial and it may seem a bit of an imposition after your long journey from Lewes. Look out, in just over a quarter of a mile, for a signed footpath going off to the left, just alongside Hill Place Farm, and now follow this path, more of a track, to another bridge over the old line. At the time of writing the old line was still covered by landfill to the left, but was clearly defined to the right and, again, access is out of the question. So return to the B2110, turn left and follow it downhill to the roundabout; take the first exit left then turn immediately left again along a road that shortly passes underneath the splendid brick-built Imberhorne Viaduct, the undoubted engineering highlight of the Lewes-East Grinstead line. As soon as you have passed under the viaduct turn right onto a concrete path that goes steeply uphill, rising to the level of the old line and then above it. There is no access to the old line but you can look down on it and stay parallel with it. Shortly the old line is seen to reach East Grinstead station and the existing London line; the path skirts the right-hand edge of the station car park and arrives at a footbridge over the railway, which you can use to gain access to the existing station. The chapter devoted to the Three Bridges-Groombridge line gives directions to the town centre from here, but if you are seeking refreshment, there is a large Sainsbury's, including café, very close to the station!

Walkers welcome on this section of the Horsted Keynes-Ardingly line.

WALK 10 - **THREE BRIDGES TO GROOMBRIDGE**

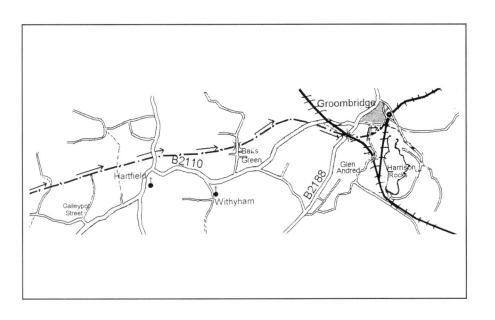

Full steam ahead on the Three Bridges-Groombridge line just west of East Grinstead.

WALK 10 - **THREE BRIDGES TO GROOMBRIDGE**

Length:	17.5 miles.
Start:	Three Bridges station.
Finish:	Groombridge station.
Public Transport:	Regular trains serving Three Bridges on the London-Brighton/Horsham line; regular buses (MB) serving Groombridge on the Tunbridge Wells-East Grinstead-Three Bridges route.
Refreshments:	Crawley Down (P,S); East Grinstead (P,C,S); Forest Row (P,C,S); Hartfield (P,C,S); Groombridge (P,C,S).
Conditions:	This is a wonderful and immensely satisfying walk, with almost all of the old line available for walkers using the Worth Way and Forest Way footpaths which are exceedingly well signposted throughout. The scenery is very attractive and amenities and public transport links are plentiful. It should be makeable by most fit walkers in a single day but East Grinstead provides an obvious stopping place should you wish to break it down into two days.

History

The line linking Three Bridges and Groombridge was in fact part of a route that ran between Three Bridges and Tunbridge Wells in Kent, albeit the route did not open all at once. The section between Three Bridges and East Grinstead was built by the East Grinstead Railway Company and opened on 9th July 1855; the London, Brighton & South Coast Railway operated it and duly acquired it from the East Grinstead Railway Company. It was then local enterprise, in the form of the East Grinstead, Groombridge and Tunbridge Wells Railway Company that led to the extension to Tunbridge Wells which opened on 1st October 1866. There had been a number of delays in the commencement of services on the line, and the press eventually got so tired of waiting that they failed to report the actual opening!

The first station out of Three Bridges was Rowfant. Even now the site of the station seems quite remote, but it was opened in the days when land was given to a new railway company in return for the provision of a station on the estate. The land through which the line passed here was given by an American fur trader named Curtis Miranda Lampson and the station was given to Lampson in return, including a shelter for

Lampson's coachmen! The next station was Grange Road, which was sited in Crawley Down, and which for a number of years had a rather longer name - Grange Road For Crawley Down And Turners Hill. It was opened in 1860. The next station, at East Grinstead, was initially a terminus, but when the Tunbridge Wells extension was opened the station was resited, and became a two-level station, the upper level - now the car park of the current station - being that used by the Three Bridges line, and the lower level used by trains coming from Lewes and going forward to London. Heading south-east from East Grinstead, the next station was Forest Row, the busiest of the intermediate stations on the route; indeed, in the final years of the line, a number of London commuters were using this station, and some trains from London to East Grinstead were in fact extended to terminate here. The next station along the line was Hartfield, which despite the modest size of the community it served boasted a goods yard loop that could hold 13 wagons. One bizarre incident in the history of the line was in June 1868 when a driver hauling a cattle train near Hartfield was warned that there was a bull on the track. Unfortunately the axle of one of the trucks broke and a derailment resulted. The bull heard what he evidently believed to be the sound of female cows in distress and charged towards the source of the noise so rapidly that the driver, hurrying for his footplate, broke his collar-bone. The next stop was Withyham, with its unfussy slate roof and small goods yard, and then came Groombridge preceded by the junction with lines for Eridge, Lewes (via Uckfield) and Polegate (via Heathfield) to the south, and London (via Oxted) to the north. Beyond Groombridge the line moved from Sussex into Kent. There were then two further intermediate stations between Groombridge and Tunbridge Wells, namely High Rocks Halt, opened in 1907 and designed to cater for visitors to the splendid rocky outcrops hereabouts, and Tunbridge Wells West, a splendid construction which with its clock tower and ornamental ceiling is now a listed building.

Bradshaw's 1890 timetable shows five direct services between Three Bridges and Tunbridge Wells each weekday, plus a couple of trains from Three Bridges to East Grinstead with the possibility of going forward to Tunbridge Wells on a train leaving 40-45 minutes later. There were two through trains on Sundays. The timing of the Sunday trains was curious; if you missed the 9.30am from Three Bridges, you would have to wait until 8.25pm for the only other train of the day. Some consolation could be derived from the fact that the 9.30am took an hour to cover the twenty and a quarter miles to Tunbridge Wells whereas the later train sped to its destination in a cool 54 minutes. However, the line grew in popularity and usage, and by 1955, the line west from East Grinstead to Three Bridges had 17 weekly and 10 Sunday return journeys. But this was pre-Beeching; being a cross-country connection or lateral line, not a route in and out of London, it was an obvious candidate for Beeching's hit list, and the part of the route between Three Bridges and Groombridge closed on 1st January 1967. Ironically East Grinstead was Dr Beeching's home town for many years and on what was the old line there is now a street in East Grinstead called Beeching Way! The section of line between Tunbridge Wells and Groombridge did survive, and in fact trains ran direct from Tunbridge Wells via Groombridge down to Eridge, the Groombridge-Eridge section part of a link line between Groombridge and Uckfield which had been served by rail from Lewes since 1858. The whole of the section from Tunbridge Wells to Eridge via Groombridge (the section between Groombridge and Eridge wholly in East Sussex) closed in July 1985. However the section from Tunbridge Wells to Groombridge was revived some years later and became the Spa Valley Railway, with the hope of an extension to Eridge; the section from Eridge to Uckfield still survives on the Southern network as part of the London-Edenbridge-Uckfield line. The section of defunct line from Three Bridges to Groombridge has been superbly restored for leisure use and offers some of the best disused railway walking in Sussex, using sections of the Worth Way and Forest Way footpaths.

Walking the Line

Your walk starts at Three Bridges railway station. Turn right out of the main station exit and then immediately right to pass under the existing railway, bearing immediately right again to follow Station Hill. Ignore a signed public footpath soon going off to the left, but a little way beyond, just a few hundred yards from Three Bridges station, look for the cycleway signpost (signed East Grinstead) pointing along a footpath to the left, and turn left to join this cycleway. Immediately to the right, opposite the junction of Station Hill and the cycleway, you can see the point at which the old line left the existing one. Follow the cycleway, which overlaps with Worth Way at this point, and you will at once find yourself following the course of the old line; initially the surroundings are distinctly suburban, but the going is very pleasant. Continue along the course of the old line, notwithstanding the signposting of the Worth Way away from the line, and follow it on until you reach an overbridge with a flight of steps built onto the side of it. You have to leave the old line here as the M23, which cannot be crossed here, lies immediately beyond, so climb up the steps, turn right and proceed southwards from the bridge along the footpath which soon emerges into Saxon Road on a modern housing estate. Go forward to join Saxon Road then turn shortly left into Harold Road and then almost immediately right into Alfred Close, soon arriving at the Worth Way again. Turn left to follow what is an excellent footpath eastwards over the M23 then north-eastwards past Worth Lodge Farm. Just by the farm buildings the Worth Way (your way) veers right, but a lane leads off to the left and by detouring along it you soon reach a pair of gates on either side. It is possible to go through the left-hand gate into the field and follow the course of the old line - obvious from the remains of the redbrick bridge just beyond the gates - back to the M23, but you're then forced back to the gates. There's little point in continuing beyond the gates along the course of the old line, as the way forward onto Turners Hill Road is obstructed by a fence, so return to the Worth Way and follow it to Turners Hill Road. The course of the old line is followable with the eyes for much of this section of walk so you won't really miss anything by not being able to walk it.

A crossing of the Three Bridges-Groombridge line near Forest Row.

Having reached Turners Hill Road via the Worth Way, turn left and almost immediately right along the signed Worth Way path. You are now on the old line and will remain on it or immediately adjacent to it for a good couple of miles; you've left the housing behind and the going has become delightfully rural. In less than a mile you cross Wallage Lane and pass the former Rowfant station. From here to the B2028 overbridge, the going is straightforward and really delightful, the Worth Way running either on or immediately next to the course of the old line throughout. Beyond the B2028 overbridge, you enter the built-up area known as Crawley Down and, as the course of the old line has now been built on, you are forced just to the south of the line to proceed to the centre of the village. There is no trace whatsoever of Grange Road Station which was sited here. The course of the old line is inaccessible for half a mile or so beyond the centre of Crawley Down, new housing having covered all traces of its course. Following the excellent Worth Way signposting, go along Burleigh Way north-eastwards away from the parade of shops, turn right off Burleigh Way into Woodland Drive and then turn shortly left into Hazel Way, still observing the Worth Way signposts. Walk along Hazel Way for some distance, then, as it bends slightly left, turn right into Cob Close which leads to a footpath that in turn goes forward to rejoin the course of the old line. Now it is a very easy and delightful two-mile walk to East Grinstead through unspoilt countryside with a mixture of woodland and open fields around you. You then enter East Grinstead and skirt the northern edge of the station car park, which is the site of the high level section of the old station, your aim being the top end of the car park (1). As you pass the car park, look out for a rather florid signpost beside your path; just by

this signpost is what appears to be a path leading off to the left, accessible by crossing over a low metal bar. This "path" is in fact the old St Margaret's Loop, a loop line that was opened in 1884 with the aim of linking the Three Bridges-Tunbridge Wells line with the still extant East Grinstead-Victoria line, and closed in 1967. It is not a designated right of way, albeit it is marked on some street plans as such, and in fact although there are no manmade obstructions to progress along it, there are two reasons why you shouldn't follow it. The first is that while progress is initially quite easy, it becomes very much tougher and more frustrating, with varying obstructions including thick undergrowth, fallen trees, accumulations of bricks and other debris, and often deep puddles and glutinous mud; it is in a deep shady cutting, and beyond the second of two fine tall brick overbridges, progress becomes all but impossible and there's no means of escape other than retracing your steps. In any

An ornate signpost beside the Three Bridges-Groombridge line at Forest Row.

event you can't get out at the other end, as the loop merges with the extant line. The second reason for not following it is perhaps more cogent: although not officially designated as such, it is unofficially regarded as an important nature conservation area, effectively a wildlife corridor and home to a large variety of species, with human intrusion unwelcome. If you are desperate to inspect the loop, you could perhaps follow it as far as the first overbridge, the going being fairly tolerable over that stretch, then retreat to the main path and walk to the top end of the car park at (1) above. Take the far eastern exit from the car park into Grosvenor Road, and follow it briefly, then turn very shortly left into Crescent Road. Follow it to Park Road and having detoured left to inspect the line beneath what is the first overbridge, cross straight over into Maypole Road and follow it to London Road. Turn left into London Road to pass over what is the second overbridge, then go first right into Lingfield Road and second right into Charlwood Road, turning right opposite Wellington Town Road along a path which soon crosses the loop and provides a final chance to view it. You can see just what a jungle it is. Now retrace your steps to (1) above.

To progress further, whether you've decided to make the above detour or not, you need to get to (1) above and turn southwards from this point, your journey along the Worth Way now at an end and East Grinstead to be negotiated. Make your way over the footbridge across the existing railway, descending to the forecourt area of the existing railway station, and walk down to the roundabout junction (there's a useful Sainsbury's immediately to your right, including a café). If you wished to stay absolutely faithful to the old line as it proceeded on towards Forest Row, you would need to turn left (not **hard** left) at the roundabout onto the verge on the far side of the A22 inner ring road heading just north of east, and follow alongside this road. Ironically it is called Beeching Way after the man responsible for shutting the old line. There is no pavement and it is a potentially quite dangerous walk alongside what is an extremely busy road, eventually arriving at a roundabout immediately across which you will see the signed Forest Way path. A much safer and pleasanter alternative is to go straight over the roundabout beyond the station forecourt to enter Railway Approach (the next exit round from the A22 ring road heading east) and follow this road to its junction with London Road. Turn right into London Road, East Grinstead's principal shopping street, and follow it to a T-junction at the end. Turn left and follow the road past the church and a number of fine old houses and shops - really the nicest part of the town - eventually reaching the roundabout at the end of Beeching Way mentioned above. The Forest Way path is signposted immediately to your right, and you now proceed along this path; you'll in fact be following the Forest Way almost all the way to Groombridge at the end of your walk. Initially the path runs downhill and just to the right of the course of the old line, but soon finds itself following the old line, the walking easy and very enjoyable. Soon you have left the suburbs of East Grinstead behind and you now head south-eastwards into open countryside, enjoying really excellent views, particularly to the right, where woodland dominates the skyline. In two and a half miles from East Grinstead you arrive at the crossing of the A22, just a quarter of a mile from Forest Row. By detouring right and following the A22 you will soon reach the centre of this sizeable and quite sprawling village, with its good range of shops and refreshment opportunities; sadly the noise of the A22 London-Eastbourne road, which cuts through the village, does little to add to its charm. Returning to the course of the old line, use the pelican crossing to negotiate your way across the A22 and continue your walk. To begin with you follow a driveway parallel with the old line, which follows an embankment above you to your right; it is possible to gain access to the embankment but is hardly worth the effort as the undergrowth and vegetation along the embankment make progress either way impracticable. In any case, as you continue along the driveway, you will notice that the course of the old line to the right soon leaves the embankment behind and proceeds through the middle of an industrial estate, passing the site of the former Forest Row station. Its course through the estate is fairly obvious. The driveway rises and now you need to look out for and take a track that forks to the right, signed Forest Way, then having passed just to the left of the far end of the industrial estate, you soon find yourself back on the course of the old line, heading for Hartfield.

The walk to Hartfield is quite delightful; it is four miles of disused railway walking at its very best, the Forest Way path sticking to the old line throughout. To begin with there is housing beside the route, but once clear of Forest Row you find yourself out in really charming countryside, with woodland (the fringes of Ashdown Forest) to your right and meadows bordering the infant River Medway to your left. Initially you continue south-eastwards, but having shaken off the built-up area at the eastern edge of Forest Row, you begin to head north-eastwards, enjoying excellent views to the fine Ashdown House which lies on the left (north) side of the old line. This section of route is particularly popular with cyclists and walkers, so do not expect to be on your own! Four miles from Forest Row you pass underneath the B2026 Maresfield-Edenbridge road, with clear signposting that indicates the village of Hartfield just a quarter of a mile to the south, and you wish to make the detour to visit it. Hartfield is a beautiful village, attracting many visitors because it is in this area that the Winnie The Pooh books of A.A. Milne were set, and there is a shop in the village which sells a variety of Pooh merchandise. The village boasts a good shop and pub, and a fine church with a magnificent spire which you can clearly see from the old line even if you decide not to visit the village. Directly beyond the access path for the B2026 you will see the old station building of Hartfield which is now in private ownership and inaccessible; the Forest Way proceeds round the left-hand edge of the old station area, allowing quite beautiful views to the adjoining meadows, and shortly rejoins the course of the old line.

Another lovely stretch of old line follows, and there is the additional delight of views to the rather wider Medway to your left. In just under 2 miles you cross a metalled road and pass the rather inelegantly-named hamlet of Balls Green, at which the old Withyham station building was situated; Withyham, with its picturesque church and pub, lies about half a mile to the south-west. Beyond Balls Green the Forest Way, remaining faithful to the old line, hugs right up to the Medway and the going is still very pleasant. The first sign that you are nearing the end of your walk along the course of the old line comes when, just before Ham Bridge where the old line crossed over the B2110 Forest Row-Tunbridge Wells road, the Forest Way path leaves the old line and drops down to the B2110 to get round the former bridge crossing. It is open to you to follow the old line and then descend quite steeply to meet the road, but that option is perhaps best left for the purist! Cross the road and rejoin the Forest Way immediately opposite.

Two lovely views of the Three Bridges-Groombridge line between Forest Row and Hartfield in the valley of the still young river Medway.

You soon return to the course of the old line but your stay on it is short-lived, as very soon the Forest Way follows a course parallel with the old line but immediately to the right of it. It was here that the old line was united briefly with the still operational Edenbridge-Uckfield line coming in from the left. Proceed along the Forest Way parallel with this line and arrive at a crossing with the B2188 Groombridge-Maresfield road, going over the road and continuing along the Forest Way. Initially it runs parallel with the Edenbridge-Uckfield line, but shortly swings left to pass underneath it, in fact just beyond the point at which the Three Bridges-Tunbridge Wells line parted from the Edenbridge-Uckfield line, going off to the left. The Forest Way now runs parallel with and just to the right of the Three Bridges-Tunbridge Wells line as far as the next road junction just a few hundred yards ahead. The old line is completely inaccessible, and no more of it is in fact walkable. When you reach the road, turn left to follow it, passing underneath the old line, now on the outskirts of Groombridge; the road goes uphill and swings round to the right, then shortly bends left, and on the bend there is a footpath leading off to the right. Take this path which almost immediately arrives at a bridge, from which you can view the old Groombridge-Eridge line (see below) and also "your" line from Three Bridges coming in to meet the Groombridge-Eridge line.

Return to the road and continue along it, now heading north along what is a residential street. You pass a little church and, heading downhill, go straight over one crossroads then shortly reach another crossroads at which you turn right into Springfield Road. Shortly you arrive at a T-junction with Station Road; turn right onto Station Road and almost immediately left to arrive at the fine old redbrick Groombridge railway station buildings. The old station building at Groombridge is now in private ownership but when you reach the building you're then signposted onto the platform which gives access, via a bridge under Station Road, to the "new" Groombridge station which serves the preserved Spa Valley Railway. This makes a fitting climax to your lovely walk from Three Bridges. At the time of writing, Groombridge, as stated above, is the western terminus of the Spa Valley Railway; the section of line going southwards to Eridge, and the junction with the extant Edenbridge-Uckfield line (part of the Southern network), is still disused. However it is likely that trains on the Spa Valley Railway will have started to run to Eridge by the time this book appears, and in any case, trains use part of the line on to Eridge to reverse for the return journey towards Tunbridge Wells West. Accordingly you should not try to get down off the platform at Groombridge to follow the line southwards to Eridge.

To pick up a bus back to Three Bridges or on to Tunbridge Wells, retrace your steps along Station Road and simply continue to the main road, turning right to shortly arrive at the bus stop for Three Bridges (near side) or Tunbridge Wells (across the road). If you've time in hand, there's a reasonable range of amenities in the village and by continuing along the main road beyond the bus stop you reach the old part of the village, actually in Kent, which is charming and well worth a visit.

The very end of the Three Bridges-Groombridge line and its imminent meeting with the Spa Valley Railway.

WALK 11 - REDGATE MILL JUNCTION TO POLEGATE / STONE CROSS

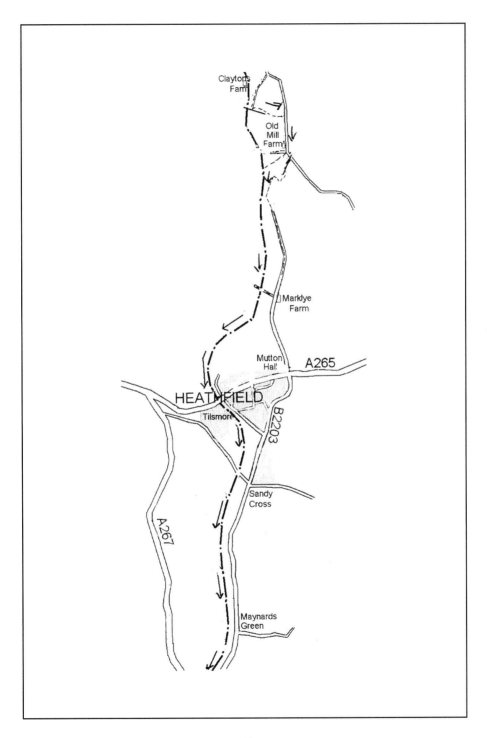

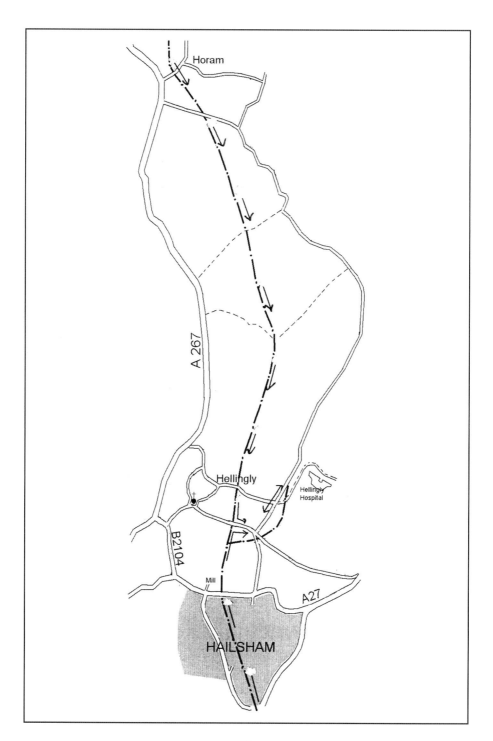

Horam

A 267

Hellingly

Hellingly
Hospital

B2104

Mill

A27

HAILSHAM

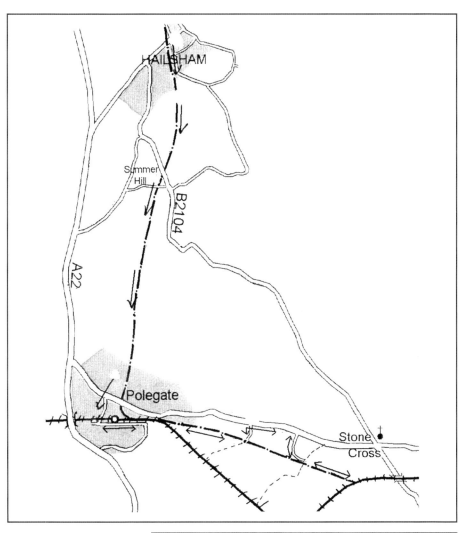

An attractive but private section of the Redgate Mill-Polegate line just north of Rotherfield.

WALK 11 - REDGATE MILL JUNCTION TO POLEGATE / STONE CROSS

Length:	Approximately 22 miles including detours.
Start:	Boar's Head pub (between Crowborough and Eridge).
Finish:	Polegate station.
Public Transport:	Regular buses (BH) serving Boar's Head on the Brighton-Tunbridge Wells route; regular buses (SC) serving Mayfield and Heathfield on the Tunbridge Wells-Eastbourne route; regular trains serving Polegate on the Brighton-Eastbourne-Hastings line.
Refreshments:	Town Row (S); Mayfield (P,C,S); Heathfield (P,C,S); Horam (P,C,S); Hailsham (P,C,S); Polegate (P,C,S).
Conditions:	This is a superbly rewarding walk, but tough in places, and you will do well to complete it in a day. You may prefer to split it into 2 days. The first half of the walk, to just above Heathfield, is able to stay faithful to the course of the old line for much of the way, but at the cost of having to use paths and tracks that generally aren't designated rights of way and you need to refer carefully to my introductory notes. However, the second half, all the way from Heathfield to Polegate, has been turned into a walkway/cycleway known as the Cuckoo Trail. The scenery is beautiful throughout.

History

It was during the mid-1840's that a rail link was completed between London and Polegate via Lewes, and on 14th May 1849 a branch was opened between Polegate and Eastbourne to the south, and also one linking Polegate with Hailsham to the north. The Polegate to Hailsham branch was extended northwards to Heathfield, this extension opening on 5th April 1880, and on 1st September of the same year there opened a further extension to Redgate Mill to link with the Tunbridge Wells to Uckfield line (via Groombridge and Eridge) that had been completed in August 1868, albeit trains had run between Tunbridge Wells and Groombridge since October 1866. This enabled trains to run direct from Tunbridge Wells to Eastbourne and back. A 1924 timetable shows nine trains a day doing the full journey in both direction on weekdays, and three on Sundays, while a number of other trains made shorter journeys which might start or finish at Hailsham or Heathfield, the two principal intermediate stations. The journey was exceedingly slow, and despite the distance being less than 30 miles from end to end, the average journey time was about an hour and a half with some journeys being a good deal longer; the 4.34pm from Eastbourne, for instance, did not arrive in Tunbridge Wells West until 6.21pm. Virtually all services were operated by the London, Brighton & South Coast Railway prior to the formation of the Southern Railway in 1923, and the subsequent takeover by British Railways after World War 2. The line became known as the Cuckoo Line because of the Cuckoo Fair held at Heathfield on 14th April each year, with many fairgoers naturally arriving by train.

The description of the line itself goes from north to south, to maintain consistency with the description of the walk which works better in that direction; the northern half is more demanding, and better done earlier in the walk than later. There were six intermediate stations between Redgate Mill and Polegate. The first station was Rotherfield & Mark Cross, three quarters of a mile from Rotherfield, one mile from Mark Cross, and in fact built between the two places in the smaller village of Town Row! Set in a beautiful rural location amongst rolling hills and coniferous woodland, it boasted a goods yard that handled a considerable amount of merchandise, notably coal; it has since been splendidly restored into a private dwelling and makes a delightful spectacle for the railway rambler. Next was Mayfield, an elegant construction with gables and tile-hanging, and much of it still standing today. Thirdly came Heathfield, serving

The rather formidable-looking tunnel mouth at Heathfield on the Redgate Mill-Polegate line.

the largest community on the line between Redgate Mill Junction and Polegate; it was advertised on station boards as Heathfield Cross In Hand, the appendage Cross In Hand referring to a smaller village just to its west. When the railway came to Heathfield the village was tiny, but the advent of the line resulted in considerable building development; the station, also lavishly built, boasted a goods yard and fully glazed footbridge, but there is no trace of the station building now. At Heathfield was the longest tunnel on the line, running to 266 yards - it is still accessible today - and it was a couple of miles north of Heathfield that there was a serious derailment in September 1897, resulting in the death of the driver and a number of injuries. South of Heathfield, the next station was Horam, initially known as Horeham Road for Waldron, then Horeham Road & Waldron, then Waldron & Horeham Road, and finally Horam! Considering the small size of the community it served, it was another impressive construction with tile-hung exterior and much ornamental plasterwork, but again cannot be seen today. The next was Hellingly, a rural station which until 1899 served the needs of what was a small village and the agricultural community surrounding it. However in that year, construction work started on the huge East Sussex Asylum, as it was known at that time (later to be known as the Hellingly Mental Hospital), and to facilitate the building of the asylum a branch line of a mile and a quarter was built from the station. When the asylum opened in 1903, the branch line was acquired and subsequently electrified by the local council; the line was used to transport both patients and coal for the boilers and generators that were used by the institution and which in

A delightful section of the Redgate Mill-Polegate line between Horam and Hellingly.

turn provided power for the electric locomotive. Notwithstanding the line's closure, Hellingly station building has been well preserved and remains a memorable feature of the walk. The last station before Polegate was Hailsham, a sizeable station with a goods yard and shed which were enlarged towards the end of the 19th century, but there is no trace of the station building today.

Although British Rail streamlined operations and improved frequency of services, the line became a victim of Dr Beeching, with the section between Redgate Mill Junction and Hailsham shutting on 13th June 1965 and that between Hailsham and Polegate closing on 8th September 1968. The section between Tunbridge Wells and Eridge via Groombridge closed on 6th July 1985 but the line linking Edenbridge and Uckfield via Eridge still survives (see the Three Bridges-Groombridge chapter) as does the section between Polegate and Eastbourne. Fortunately a magnificent initiative by East Sussex County Council saw the whole section between Heathfield and Polegate, including the Heathfield Tunnel, converted during the 1990's into a walkway and cycleway called, fittingly enough, the Cuckoo Trail. The remainder of the old line is still virtually all in private hands, but only comparatively small sections have been built on and it would be good to think that most of it could be made available for recreational use in the course of time.

Walking The Line

Getting to the start of the old railway walk at Redgate Mill Junction is easier than it may look. You need to get off the bus at the hamlet of Boarshead, on the A26 between Crowborough and Tunbridge Wells about a mile south-west of Eridge station; leave the A26 using the road on the east side (right side if alighting from the bus from Crowborough) and immediately you reach a T-junction at which you turn right to arrive at the Boar's Head pub, then follow the road south-eastwards away from the pub. The road proceeds pleasantly on past Cherrytree Farm in delightful mostly wooded countryside, then veers quite sharply north-eastwards and drops down to arrive at the extant Edenbridge-Eridge-Uckfield line. When you reach it, turn right at the road junction, passing under the bridge, and almost immediately to your left you'll see the embankment bearing the old line away from the extant line at the start of its journey to Polegate. This is Redgate Mill Junction, a delightfully quiet spot, and you will feel a very long way from the sprawling Eastbourne conurbation of which Polegate is part. You can't join the embankment to the left, and although you can scramble onto the course of the line heading coastwards, using a crude path a little further on and trekking through the rough grass, your way forward is blocked by fragile wooden fencing. So return to the road and follow it round to the right, past Redgate Mill Farm, going uphill. As the road reaches the top of the rise and bends slightly left, there's a gate in the hedge to the right; pass through the gate and drop down to the obvious course of the old line at the bottom, then follow it south-eastwards, roughly parallel with the road. It's good to be on the old line so soon, but as you get close to the next road crossing, your way forward is blocked by a securely fenced overbridge, so as you reach it, bear half-left across the field to a gate and exit onto the road. Turn right to follow the road very briefly, but just before the road rises to cross the old line you can bear left onto a track which almost immediately joins the course of the old line. Proceed through a field initially, then enter very attractive woodland and continue along the course of the old line, shortly reaching a line of wire fencing (1) which appears to bar your route.

Now you have your first decision to make. Beyond the wire fence the land is private, accessible only by climbing an adjacent wooden fence, and when you reach the other end of this section of land there's a gate to surmount. Therefore you should seek permission before proceeding; if you do not have permission, you continue at your own risk, and you may decide you would rather not attempt it. If you do proceed, drop down to the right and climb over the wooden fence, beyond which, having crossed a footbridge, it's easy to regain the old line. Delightful walking now follows along a clear

Hellingly station on the Redgate Mill-Polegate line.

path through lovely woodland. At length you emerge from the woods and get within sight of a storage barn built on the course of the old line, but a path has been constructed round the right-hand edge of the barn along a bank above it, and beyond you can continue along the course of the old line to reach two gates. Go through or over the left-hand one, but beyond it, there is no possibility of following the old line for the short distance to the old Rotherfield & Mark Cross station building, so turn right onto what is a public footpath and follow it uphill to reach the B2100 at its junction with Chant Lane. Turn left to follow the B2100 downhill to the rather sprawling village of Town Row, passing under the old railway bridge and turning first left to view the private but splendidly kept old Rotherfield & Mark Cross station building, with immaculate garden. If you decide not to attempt this section, backtrack from the point at (1) above to the road, turn right and follow it for a very short distance to a crossroads, turning right here and following the road which after a mile arrives at Town Row and reaches the old station.

Whichever route you've taken to reach the old station, walk down the road to the B2100, join it briefly then go straight on in the same direction into Yew Tree Lane. The old line is immediately to your right here, and the embankment looks easy enough to get on to, but the course of the old line is then swallowed up by the back gardens of houses. Pass the useful shop then carry on along Yew Tree Lane, soon arriving at a junction with Sheriff's Lane which goes off to the right; from a gate just before the junction you can see the course of the old line, but you can't meaningfully follow it in either direction, the old bridge crossing of Sheriff's Lane securely fenced off. Continue along Yew Tree Lane beyond the junction, soon reaching a signed footpath going off to the right which almost immediately arrives at the course of the old line, but again it can't be followed far in either direction, so return to Yew Tree Lane and keep along it in a south-easterly direction until the road bends to the left. On this bend there's a lane leading off to the right, down to a bridge carrying the old line; at the time of writing the lane was advertised as leading to a trout farm. Follow the lane then as you reach the bridge, climb up the embankment - it's not too steep - to join the course of the old line, and turn left to follow it south-eastwards, soon veering south-westwards.

You can now enjoy some excellent woodland walking along the old line; it isn't designated as a right of way but there are no prohibitions on access, there are neither manmade nor natural obstructions, and indeed in many places a crude path has been cut, suggesting that efforts have been made to turn this into a proper recreational path. You're warned at one overbridge crossing of the dangers of falling masonry, then shortly enter quite a long tunnel under the A267 Tunbridge Wells-Polegate road. You emerge from the tunnel with a steep cutting on both sides, and the village of Argos Hill immediately beyond the top of the cutting to the right. The path, such as it is, tends to become more vague just here, but keep going, and soon you'll find yourself going uphill to meet a crossing track. At first sight your way forward would seem to be obstructed by a fence, but by looking carefully you will see a stile in the fence onto the track, and another one immediately beyond the track; having crossed the stile you walk gently downhill to find yourself on the obvious course of the old line once more. This is now really lovely walking, with beautiful countryside particularly to your left, and a proper path more or less throughout. Indeed as you reach an overbridge crossing of Bassetts Lane you'll actually be following what is a recently designated public bridleway, the only section of old line between Redgate Mill Junction and Heathfield to be a designated right of way. The A267 runs more or less parallel with you to the right. Keep on along the course of the old line, until the path ends at a road, in fact the road leading from the A267 to the village of Mayfield; turn right to follow this road to the A267, and bear left to follow beside the A267, using a sort of "hard shoulder" to the left.

Your walk alongside the A267, the Mayfield bypass at this point, is hardly the most interesting or enjoyable part of the day, but it is at least faithful to the course of the old line, which is immediately alongside and to the left of the hard shoulder you are following. It is however rather sad to see how what traces of the lovely old railway that there were have had to be sacrificed to facilitate the construction of the new road. It is something of a relief to arrive at the junction with Fir Toll Road which goes off to the right; immediately opposite this right turn, you turn left, up the steps, then as you reach the top of the steps, you cross the course of the old line which is still quite hard to discern and impossible to join in either direction. You now need to bear right to continue downhill along Station Road, but it's possible to detour left along Station

Approach to view the old Mayfield station building. Having taken a look at it, return to follow Station Road downhill, keeping the course of the old line to your right. At the bottom you reach a junction, where you shouldn't veer right to the roundabout, but go straight over into Newick Lane; the old line can't be picked up immediately beyond the junction here, as it is lost in the back gardens of properties. Although your way forward is along Newick Lane, part of cycle route 21, you could turn left along West Street to access the centre of Mayfield, a lovely village with an excellent range of amenities.

The next part of the walk as far as the outskirts of Heathfield incorporates some good sections of old line, but they are all private with no public right of access. I have made it clear below where you may encounter problems, and I cannot emphasize strongly enough that if you wish to walk them safely and legally you should obtain permission; if you want to take the risk and walk them without permission, that is up to you, but neither my publisher nor I can accept responsibility for the consequences. If permission isn't forthcoming and you do not fancy taking the risk, you may be best advised to cut your losses and follow cycle route 21 which is well signposted, walking along Newick Lane to just beyond Old Mill Farm then turning right onto a path which takes you as far as Marklye Farm. Here you join Marklye Lane which takes you to a crossroads junction, and turning right here you'll arrive in Heathfield. Proceed along the main street then turn left into Station Road and very shortly fork right into Station Approach, here picking up the route description at (4) below.

Assuming you want to stick to the old line, or as much of it as you can, walk briefly up Newick Lane, and shortly beyond the properties referred to above, but just before a sharp left bend, there's a signed footpath to the right. This brings you to a bridge over the old line, which is in a steep cutting below you. At the time of writing construction work was going on hereabouts, but it was possible to scramble down the bank to join the old line, and follow it on round the side of a large shed to a junction with a farm lane going off to the left (2). However, this is clearly private land and not only should you seek permission to walk it but future construction work may mean the bank and indeed the course of the old line becomes inaccessible. If you decide not to take the risk, or it's inaccessible anyway, the alternative is to stay on Newick Lane as it bends round to the left then right, just south of east, as far as Woodhay, a house on the right. You could then turn right through the gate just before Woodhay and follow the farm lane to reach the old line at point (2) above, and could of course backtrack towards Mayfield along the course of the old line if you wished. However it should be emphasized that the farm lane from Woodhay to point (2) is private, with warning signs to that effect, so you should seek permission first.

Whichever way you reached point (2), it is now possible for you to follow the obvious course of the old line for about half a mile, and it is lovely walking, with fine views through the trees to the surrounding countryside, albeit it's somewhat rough in places and again it is not a designated right of way. In about half a mile you reach a crossing

A chance to relax on the Redgate Mill-Polegate line south of Hailsham.

track with a gate to your left (3); although it is possible to continue a short distance beyond the crossing track through the trees, your way does become obstructed by fencing so you'll need to backtrack. Pass through the gate at (3) above and head in a roughly easterly direction across the field to a gate which you cross. Beyond it you should be able to see Newick Lane, and you now head for that lane, passing shortly through another gate and entering another field, exiting it through a gate to arrive at Newick Lane. For the avoidance of doubt, none of this field-walking is along designated rights of way. Now turn right to follow Newick Lane briefly, soon reaching the buildings of Old Mill Farm where the road bends sharply left; immediately beyond this left bend, turn right along the plinth-signed bridleway, not following the signposted cycle route 21 (unless you wish to keep to it, in view of the obstructions you face on the old line itself, in which case follow the instructions for route 21 given above), then turn almost immediately left up a road signposted St Quentins. You approach a bridge carrying the old line, and just before it turn left up a slipway track which arrives on the old line. It's actually possible to turn right to follow it almost back to the point where you had to leave it previously, but there's no chance of a link because of the fencing, so retrace your steps along the old line - a very clear, easy walk here - and continue past the point where you just joined it.

Very shortly your progress appears to be halted by some private buildings that are actually on the course of the old line, but use a track to veer round to the left of them. Follow the track briefly, climbing gently, but as it swings further to the left, away from the course of the old line, turn right into the trees - there's no path - and aim for a field that becomes visible to your half-left. Follow the right-hand field edge, remaining parallel with the old line which is clearly discernible beyond the buildings referred to above but separated from it by a fence. Beyond the field continue in the same direction through the trees, remaining parallel with the old line and keeping the fence immediately to your right; there's no path here as such at all, but it's not difficult to stay with the fence. Proceed gently downhill and at length the fence gives out, enabling you to rejoin the course of the old line. Progress is now more straightforward, but I should remind you that you are still on private land, and although your mostly wooded walk is easy in parts, there are occasions when you do need to pick your way round fallen trees and other vegetation. You pass very close to Orchard House and out of respect for the owners' privacy it is suggested that as you approach the overbridge which bears a crossing footpath, you leave the old line and walk up to the path, cross it and then return to the old line on the other side.

Beyond Orchard House, the going remains easy, until you arrive at a rather formidable looking metal fence construction clearly intended to prevent those coming the other way (up what is a designated right of way beyond the fence) progressing further! It is however quite easy to get round the obstruction, turning left just before it and scrambling over the rough ground to reach a dirt track; turn right to follow the track over a shallow ditch, then bear round to the right to pick up the old line on the other side of the metal fencing. This is a key moment on your walk, as from now on, save for occasional deviations resulting from modern development, you can follow the old line all the way to Polegate on designated rights of way. With a spring in your step, you now proceed along an excellent path through beautiful woodland, passing through a small country park called Millennium Green, and entering Heathfield Tunnel. It isn't as

Path furniture on the Redgate Mill-Polegate line not far from Polegate.

dramatic as some other tunnels you may meet on your Sussex disused railway walking, for although it's quite long, it's been resurfaced and also illuminated. Emerging from the tunnel, you can see a dead end ahead in the form of a blocked-up overbridge, so use steps to climb up to a road; at the time of writing there was a useful café immediately on the other side of the road. To reach the many amenities of Heathfield you need to turn left into Station Approach and very shortly left into Station Road which brings you to the main street, but to continue along the route you should bear right and follow Station Approach (4) then take the next left turn. Follow this road down to a junction, turning left and almost immediately right to rejoin the old line, which, as you can see by a look to your left, is impassable beyond the blocked-up overbridge referred to above by virtue of an industrial estate.

Now you can look forward to 11 miles of virtually unbroken walking on the old line, along the Cuckoo Trail which caters for both walkers and cyclists; the concrete surface may be hard on the feet in every sense but it makes for quick and mud-free walking, a treat after all the undergrowth north of Heathfield! Almost at once you can see how much time and effort has been invested into the project by the local council, with excellent signposting including very helpful mileposts, firm concrete surfacing, and lineside benches with most artistic wood carvings. Initially there's a suburban feel but soon after the Ghyll Road crossing the houses relent. A crossing track provides a possible detour eastwards to the splendidly-named Runt-in-Tun pub, and appropriately enough you pass over Runts Farm Bridge nearby, going forward to cross Tubwell Lane at the small village of Maynard's Green. There is a contrasting scene between left and right: to the right, delightful rolling fields and woods, and to the left, the busy B2203 road, the noise from which can seem quite intrusive. Soon afterwards you arrive at Horam, passing the site of the station, and your route hereabouts very briefly has to deviate from the course of the old line, although the signposting is excellent and the village, which is easily accessed, enjoys a good range of amenities. The next section, as far as Hellingly, is the loveliest on the whole of this walk. Striking out south-eastwards from Horam, you are able beyond Horebeech Lane to leave the traffic noise as well as housing behind, and enjoy quite beautiful scenery from the comfort of your immaculate path. You pass through a lovely area of refreshing woodland which provides glorious colours in spring, then after crossing the quaintly-named Cattle Creep Bridge and going under the fine triple-arched Woodhams Bridge, you find you're joined by the pretty Cuckmere River which is to your left. You veer gently from south-east to south-west and pass under Shawpits Bridge, then shortly cross over the Cuckmere, the scenery around the river crossing as beautiful as any you'll encounter on your disused railway walking in Sussex. You drop down to cross Mill Lane then soon pass under Station Road and you'll immediately see the very well-preserved Hellingly station to your right.

Here, if you wish, you could make a detour to inspect the old hospital line referred to in the "History" part of the pre-amble to this chapter. I have to say that it is for the connoisseur only, as it is almost all road walking, it is a straight "out and back," and there is no evidence of the old hospital line at all. It will also add a good two and a half miles to your journey, so if you're pushed for time, I advise you not to bother with it. However, if you decide to do it, turn left just beyond the Station Road bridge and walk up the link path to meet Station Road; turn right onto the road and follow it to a crossroads, turning right here and looking out for a gated grassy track leading off almost immediately to the right. This is the course of the old line as it came up from the "main" Tunbridge Wells-Eastbourne line, but there's no way through the gate. When you eventually return to the Cuckoo Trail you can work out the approximate course the hospital branch would have taken to get here from the "main" line! Retrace your steps to the crossroads and go straight over, the road now running parallel with the course of the old line which ran through the field to your right. At the time of writing this was earmarked for development with some work having actually started, and although it was technically accessible from the bottom end just south-east of the crossroads, I recommend you stick to the road and follow the course of the old line with your eyes. Fork right onto The Drive, the old hospital approach road, and it was very shortly along here that the old line came in from the right and followed the course of The Drive all the way to the old hospital buildings where the line finished. Accordingly, just follow The Drive, past extensive new builds to the right, until you reach the old hospital buildings, then retrace your steps to the old Hellingly station and rejoin the Cuckoo Trail.

The walk from Hellingly to Hailsham is pleasant but you have lost the lovely rural feel you enjoyed north of Hellingly; initially there is countryside on both sides but in just under half a mile you have to cross the very busy Upper Horsebridge Road where a pelican pedestrian crossing is provided. Now the walking takes on a more suburban feel as the Cuckoo Trail threads a course between Manor Park Road to your right and Lansdowne Drive to your left, and goes under the Hawks Road Bridge, which feels more like a tunnel than a bridge. You then have to negotiate a large modern housing estate - again the Cuckoo Trail is well signposted through it - as you approach the centre of Hailsham. With the surroundings positively urban now, you pass under three bridges: the singularly unappealing London Road Bridge, the hardly inspiring Eastwell Bridge and finally the impressive Teinicks Bridge, a fine piece of brickwork. Beyond Teinicks Bridge you are as close as you are going to get to the centre of Hailsham, a sprawling town with an excellent range of amenities. You're now forced away from the course of the old line, being signposted left to the top (north) end of Station Road, then turn right to follow Station Road southwards (if you wish to visit Hailsham, turn instead left into North Street which leads to the High Street). The Cuckoo Trail follows Station Road to the first turning on the right, Lindfield Drive; turn right into Lindfield Drive then immediately left into Freshfield Close, very soon going forward to join the course of the old line and emerge into the countryside once more.

The going now becomes very pleasantly rural once again. It's not quite as beautiful as the Horam-Hellingly section, but it's enjoyable nonetheless. You pass under the B2104

No further explanation needed!

Ersham Road and then follow a clear south-westerly course, enjoying what are now excellent views to the South Downs, while to your left (eastwards) are the Pevensey Levels, an indication of how near the sea you are getting. The calm is somewhat rudely disturbed by the A27 Polegate bypass, crossed thankfully by a footbridge, and very soon you reach the outskirts of Polegate, arriving at a path junction. Here the cycle route 21, which has followed the old line all the way from Heathfield, goes off to the left, but you can keep going along the course of the old line until you're forced off it just below Polegate Primary School. This is the end of the walkable section of the Redgate Mill-Polegate line. Climb away from it up steps going round to the right (west) to find yourself at the top of School Lane, and walk down this road to reach the B2247; cross the road and turn left, and soon, on the right, you'll see a tangled area of vegetation behind formidable fencing. This marks the course of the old line as it continued on down to Polegate. You can't access it, though, so retrace your steps along the road past School Lane and now continue to the top of the High Street, the next turning on your left. Turn left and walk down the High Street to arrive at the station approach road which is on the left, just before the level crossing; bear left onto the approach road and you'll shortly arrive at Polegate station itself.

You could decide to call it a day here, as there are excellent rail connections from Polegate to Eastbourne, Brighton and London, but it is possible to continue on to Stone Cross using another section of old railway line. Whereas now all trains travelling from Polegate to Bexhill, Hastings and beyond must dip down into Eastbourne and then reverse out again, there was between 1846 and 1969 a line which bypassed Eastbourne altogether and proceeded in a more direct easterly direction towards Bexhill and

Hastings. Most of it is followable on foot and I recommend that if you've the time, you do it. If you decide to do it, walk through the station car park until you reach a modern block of flats in the car park itself; walk round to the left of the block, using the obvious alleyway, and shortly you'll pass fencing which is to your left, and behind which is a tangle of vegetation. This is actually the final part of the old line from Tunbridge Wells via Redgate Mill. You'll note that it appears to be aiming to the east of Polegate station; the station formerly lay a few hundred yards to the east, and it was into that old station that trains from Tunbridge Wells arrived. The vegetation isn't accessible, though, so carry on along the alleyway, going forward into Porters Lane and following it round to Station Road. Turn right into Station Road, shortly passing the old Polegate station building which is now a pub, and bear first right into Lynholm Road; straight ahead of you is the embankment bearing the old link line, which parted company from the extant Eastbourne-bound line a short way to the west (your right). It is impossible to access it, though, so head eastwards along Lynholm Road.

Follow the road for about a quarter of a mile, but look out carefully for the cycle path signpost leading off the road to the right, and take this signed cycle path route; this shortly swings left and now follows the course of the old link line, providing lovely walking with beautiful views to the South Downs. At length you reach the top of the cutting forged by the busy A22, and at the junction of paths here you need to descend the steps leading down to a crossing of this road, and cross it with immense care. Ascend the steps on the other side, and now follow a marked path which crosses the course of the old line and veers just east of north to reach the B2247 Dittons Road; the old line is impossible to join here but its course can be followed with the eyes across the field to the right as you head for Dittons Road. On reaching the road, turn right to follow it briefly, but then turn right again southwards down the next track on your right. A signed footpath leads away northwards from the road at this point, so it should be easy enough to identify the track. Follow the track, which bends left just short of a forbidding locked and barbed-wired gate, passes to the right of a pond, enters an area of new housing and arrives at a road. Cross straight over the road onto a path track which passes under a bridge (5) carrying the old line - the line again inaccessible here - and goes forward to a gate. Pass through or over the gate to enter a pleasant area of open rolling fields. You can turn right to follow beside the course of the old line along or close to the field edge, all the way back to the A22; assuming you do this, you then need to retrace your steps and, walking first uphill then down, follow beside the old line eastwards along the left-hand field edge up to the top corner of the field, from which you can see the point where the extant line from Eastbourne comes up to join the old line. Note that the thickness of the vegetation prevents you walking along the actual course of the old line up to this point. The views to the right are extensive and despite the profusion of suburban housing the backdrop of the South Downs is particularly pleasing to the eye.

You could just walk back to Dittons Road the same way from here, but you may be able to vary things a little. At the time of writing, it was possible, when you reached the top corner of the field, to negotiate some broken fencing and follow a path running up to and across the course of the old line, then down to a path (6) running parallel with the old line but on the north side. You can then turn right to follow that path, being able to detour off it to get a much closer view of the join between the old and extant line. The path arrives at a locked gate so you'll need to retrace your steps along it, but in fact you can continue along it all the way back to the north side of the bridge at (5) above, and backtrack to Dittons Road from there. If the broken fencing referred to above has been repaired and you can't get through, you can backtrack along the field edge uphill then descend and about halfway down the hill you may find a gap in the fencing with a path beyond enabling you to access the path referred to at (6) above. You can then decide whether to head eastwards to get that closer view of the join between old and extant line, or whether simply to turn left and head back to Dittons Road.

Once back at Dittons Road, it's a very short walk to the right (eastwards) to Stone Cross, the nearest village. However bus connections to Polegate and Eastbourne from here are not particularly plentiful and you may find it easier to turn left and follow it westwards, across the A22 roundabout and back to Polegate. In roughly a mile from the roundabout you'll reach the old station (now pub) which is to your left; just beyond the pub turn left into Porters Lane which brings you back to the station car park.

A fine section of the old "direct" line between Polegate and Stone Cross.

WALK 12 - **BEXHILL TO CROWHURST**

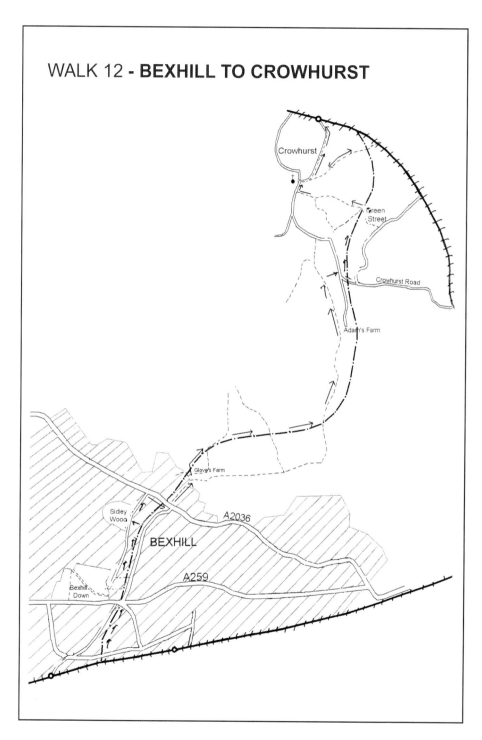

WALK 12 - BEXHILL TO CROWHURST

Length:	6 miles.
Start:	Bexhill station.
Finish:	Crowhurst station.
Public Transport:	Regular trains serving Bexhill on the Eastbourne-Hastings line; regular trains serving Crowhurst on the Tunbridge Wells-Hastings line.
Refreshments:	Bexhill (P,C,S); Sidley (P,S).
Conditions:	This is a very rewarding walk with some good sections of disused line for viewing and walking (although little of the walking is on designated rights of way), and fine scenery once you have left the sprawl of Bexhill behind. It should be able to be accomplished in half a day.

History

The Crowhurst, Sidley & Bexhill Railway Company was formed to build a four and a half mile branch from the London-Hastings line at Crowhurst, providing a "short cut" from this line to the popular seaside resort of Bexhill. The line, authorised by an Act dated 15th July 1897, was opened on 1 June 1902 and was later absorbed by the South Eastern Railway. There was one intermediate station, namely Sidley, an inland suburb of Bexhill, while the two most impressive features of the line were the Combe Haven viaduct, and the terminus, which became known as Bexhill West. The Combe Haven viaduct was a brick-built construction across the Crowhurst Valley, not far from the point at which the line branched off from the main London-Hastings line, and reached a maximum height of 70ft. Bexhill West station, as distinct from Bexhill station on the main Eastbourne-Hastings line (with which the Crowhurst-Bexhill line did not link, being

The former Bexhill West station building, the southern terminus of the Bexhill-Crowhurst line.

A profusion of hawthorn on the Bexhill-Crowhurst line just beyond Sidley.

separated simply by the width of a road!) was a huge station with a substantial concourse, a long two-faced platform, extensive sidings and a large goods depot.

The line became popular and in 1925 there were eighteen weekday departures from Crowhurst to Bexhill. However, with electrification of the Eastbourne-Hastings line which made it less immediately attractive to cut across from this line to the Hastings-Charing Cross line via Sidley and Crowhurst, traffic declined. The line did come back briefly into its own in late 1949 and early 1950 when extensive engineering work in the tunnel between West St Leonards and Warrior Square on the London-Hastings line just outside Hastings caused Hastings trains to be diverted to Bexhill West. By summer of 1958 steam trains on the line had been discontinued, being replaced by diesel multiple units, and the line finally closed to passengers on 15th June 1964 although goods traffic had ceased on 9th September 1963. The old redbrick station at Bexhill West and the remains of the Combe Haven viaduct are the most impressive features of the branch line still to survive, and the good news for walkers is that in the last few years a section of line has been converted into an attractive and well-kept footpath. It would be great to think further sections will be similarly converted in tears to come.

Walking the Line

Come out of Bexhill station by the main exit and bear left to follow Station Road just south of west, parallel with the extant Bexhill-Eastbourne line. Bear left at the end into Buckhurst Place and go straight on into Terminus Road, heading westwards until you reach the old Bexhill West station building; it has been very impressively restored, housing both an estate agent and a pub/restaurant at the time of writing, and it's worth spending a moment or two here, imagining what it must have been like when the line was running. From the station, retrace your steps very briefly and turn left up Beeching Road, just to the east of the old station building. The course of the old line runs parallel with and to the left of this road, but it is impossible to follow it because of the industrial estate on which it's built. At the end of Beeching Road, turn left and almost immediately arrive at a crossroads with the A259 Little Common Road; the embankment used by the old line can clearly be seen on the south-west segment of this crossroads. Cross over into the A269 London Road and follow this north-westwards, the course of the old line running parallel with this road just to the left, behind the backs of residential properties. It is possible to discern its course in places, but again it can't physically be followed. Just over half a mile up London Road from the crossroads, take the first left turn into Woodsgate Park, crossing over the old line; don't be fooled by the path you can see on each side of the bridge, as there's no chance of accessing it. Turn right into Buxton Road and follow it, looking out for and following a path which goes off to the right, parallel with the old line which can be followed with the eyes but again can't accessed from here. Go forward into Birch View, veering left to return to Buxton Drive, then turn right to follow it to its end and bear right again onto Ninfield Road. Drop down to cross over the course of the old line, now close to the site of Sidley station; to your right the old line has been converted into a motorcycle training area and when I visited, this was securely locked, while to your left the old line goes into a deep cutting which again can't be accessed. Accordingly, go on over the bridge and take the first left turn into Wrestwood Road, then turn almost immediately left onto a public footpath signed for Crowhurst.

Follow the path, which skirts the far western ends of St James Avenue and then shortly St James Close and proceeds north-eastwards, keeping the railway cutting to the left. There is fencing separating you from the cutting, but there is a gap in the fencing enabling you to access a crude path along the top of the cutting; that said, the path peters out just short of an overbridge, with no way back to the proper footpath, and since you can see the cutting from the footpath, it's really not worth trying to scramble down onto the old line at this point. Go forward through the field, exiting it via gates, and turn left to cross back over the old line almost at once. As soon as you've crossed the old line, turn right onto a narrow path that drops down to arrive at the old line; again there's no point in trying to access it by dropping down the bank any sooner, especially as the course of the old line is very hard to follow between the bridge and the access point. Now, at last, you're able to follow the old line along a path which is not marked on maps as a right of way but is very definitely available for walking. It's beautiful walking as well, particularly in spring when the woodland to your right is carpeted with bluebells; the surroundings are delightfully unspoilt and Bexhill and Sidley suddenly seem a long way back. Roughly a mile after joining the old line, you reach a footpath junction (1), with signed path going off to the left and a signpost for "VIEWPOINT" straight ahead along the course of the old line. The next section of old line has only fairly recently become a public path and it really is lovely walking, but sadly, and seemingly without warning, your excellent path simply stops; you can carry on along a very thin path but this soon drops steeply downhill, and peters out at the edge of a stream with no way across. One would like to think that there are plans to bridge this stream in future and extend your walk along the course of the old line, but as it is, you're forced all the way back to the point at (1) above. Turn hard right to join a clear path, in fact part of the 1066 Country Walk, which heads just east of north, roughly parallel with and to the west of the course of the old line you just followed towards the dead end. The course of the path is fairly obvious. You veer north and cross the stream that halted your progress along the course of the old line, then proceed across marshy fields, again veering very slightly east of north and aiming just to the left of the Adam's Farm buildings which you can see ahead of you to the right. There is a very conspicuous signpost which will assist you. To the right, as you reach the signpost, you can see a bank covered in vegetation which shows the obvious continuation of the course of the old line beyond the marshy fields, not accessible from here, and looking back you can see the course it took from the point where your walk along the old line ended.

Proceed northwards just below and to the left of Adam's Farm buildings on the marked path, still on the 1066 Country Walk, keeping a stream to your right. Roughly a quarter of a mile beyond Adam's Farm, you reach a footbridge over this stream; turn right to cross this footbridge and follow a path through the field, aiming for the left-hand field edge to the right of the Croucher's Farm buildings immediately ahead of you. Follow the field edge past these buildings and continue uphill, aiming for the road and veering a little left to access it, then turn hard right onto the road which although a minor road is surprisingly busy, so take care. Climb to reach a sharp left-hand bend, where you'll see a bridge over the course of the old line (2), and from here, it is possible to detour along the course of the old line back to Adam's Farm. To do this, turn right just before the bridge, down a lane, and when you reach the bottom of the incline you'll see a gate to the left; by surmounting this gate and bearing right beyond it, you'll find yourself on the course of the old line heaing southwards. Please note that this is private land and you should seek permission to walk it, referring to my introductory notes. At length the path arrives at a grassy area with vegetation behind it, just a tantalisingly short distance from the marshy fields referred to above and which you passed a short while back, but you cannot make a link with the 1066 Country Walk so you're forced back. Enjoying delightfully unspoilt surroundings, with very good views towards Hastings to your right, you'll then need to retrace your steps to the bridge at (2) above (when you reach the gate you crossed to access this piece of old line, you can't remain on its course to reach the bridge) then turn left, back onto the road.

Follow the road briefly downhill, and shortly it is possible to bear right off the road into the woods and access the course of the old line which you can follow back to the overbridge at (2) above. Then turn back and follow a path which now heads just east of north, immediately to the left of the course of the old line; though it's not shown on

A lovely stretch of the Bexhill-Crowhurst line, now available for walkers.

maps as a right of way, there is no difficulty in accessing it. Sadly, the path peters out as the course of the old line ahead becomes impossible to follow, lost in a tangle of vegetation, and you're forced to veer to the left, down to a lane leading to Sampson's Farm. Turn right to follow the lane, climbing gently, until you reach a sign (3) just before the Sampson's Farm buildings warning you that there's no footpath ahead; I suggest you turn right here to follow a path into the woods, and almost immediately you reach a bridge over the old line, half-hidden among vegetation. You could shin down the bank to the right to access the line and see what a magnificent overbridge it is, but you can't make meaningful progress in either direction, so return to the point (3) above. You now need to take the signed path leaving the Sampson's Farm lane on the opposite (north-west) side of the lane and follow it north-westwards towards Crowhurst; initially your path strikes out across fields, gradually losing height, aiming for the unmistakable landmark of Crowhurst church. You skirt the southern edge of Rackwell Wood and descend to a footbridge and path junction, then ignoring a path heading left here, cross the bridge and continue towards the church, soon arriving at a road. Turn right onto the road and at the next road junction, just beside the church, turn right into Station Road.

If you're in a hurry, you could simply follow the road to the station, about half a mile up the road. However your exploration of the very picturesque Bexhill-Crowhurst line isn't quite complete, so assuming time is on your side, almost as soon as you've entered Station Road (4)you should turn right along a farm lane, heading for farm buildings. You veer left and pass to the left of the barn ahead of you, then continue along a clear path, proceeding most pleasantly north-eastwards through fields on a hillside. You pass

A splendid overbridge crossing amid thick vegetation on the Bexhill-Crowhurst line.

a thin strip of woodland, crossing a stream, then ahead of you is a surprising sight: a splendid redbrick arch, part of the Combe Haven viaduct, and looking quite incongruous now amongst the fields and woods. Aim for the left side of the arch, climb up onto the top of it - it isn't hard - and now you're back on the old line which you can follow almost all the way back to the point where you last left it, near Sampson's Farm. However, it is very tough going in places: there's a profusion of nettles and other undergrowth, and although there are no manmade obstructions to progress, there are times when the natural obstructions force you to find a way round, using the embankment. It is worth perservering, though, as the surroundings are delightful, but disappointingly, you reach a fence which prevents further progress and forces you to retrace your steps to the redbrick arch. Before you descend from the top of the arch, look straight ahead to follow with your eyes the course the viaduct would have taken over the fields to link with the extant London Charing Cross-Hastings line; this is now very close, and in fact you'll hear the trains on that line from this point. It isn't possible to walk direct to Crowhurst station from here via the course of the old line, so descend from the arch and return to Station Road by the same route to arrive at point (4) above, and then turn right to follow Station Road to Crowhurst station. Be warned that it's quite a long slog, and there are no amenities at the station, so if you just miss one of the hourly trains, your wait for the next will seem like a very long one!

The remains of the Combe Haven viaduct at the top end of the Bexhill-Crowhurst line.

WALK 13 - **ROBERTSBRIDGE TO BODIAM**

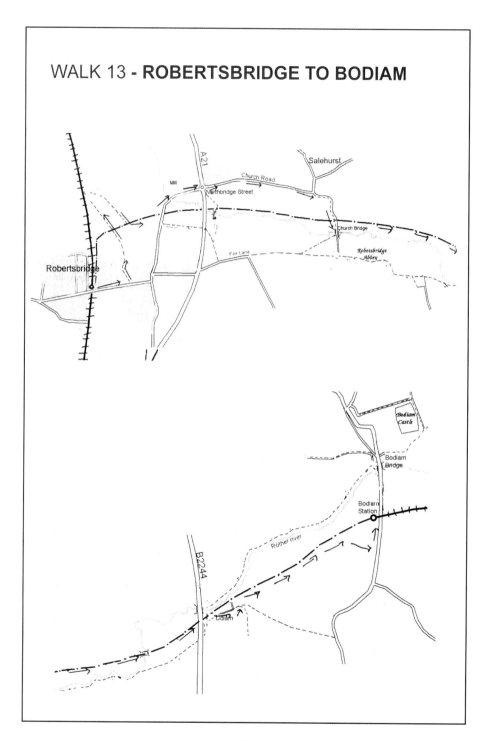

WALK 13 - **ROBERTSBRIDGE TO BODIAM**

Length:	Minimum 4 miles, maximum 8 miles.
Start:	Robertsbridge station.
Finish:	Bodiam station.
Public Transport:	Regular trains serving Robertsbridge on the London Charing Cross-Tunbridge Wells-Hastings line; trains from Bodiam to Tenterden on the preserved Kent & East Sussex Railway; regular buses (ESCC) serving Tenterden on the Ashford-Hastings route; regular buses (ESCC) from Northiam to Rye and Hastings.
Refreshments:	Robertsbridge (P,S); Salehurst (P); Bodiam (C).
Conditions:	While very little of the old line can actually be walked, you can remain within sight of it for virtually the whole way, and it is a very scenic and enjoyable walk, which shouldn't take more than a couple of hours. You should aim to do the walk when the Kent & East Sussex Railway is running, because you can then pick up a train from Bodiam; not only will this provide continuity to your exploration, but it will avoid an extra 4-mile walk.

History

The line linking Robertsbridge and Bodiam was part of a line which linked Robertsbridge, on the London-Hastings main line, with Headcorn on the London-Dover main line. Following application by the Rother Valley Railway Company, it was in 1896 that an Act was passed allowing the construction of a branch line between Robertsbridge and Tenterden, but in fact when the Light Railways Act received Royal assent in the same year, it was decided by the company to construct the line under the provisions of that Act which meant that construction costs were able to be reduced. The line opened to goods traffic on 26th March 1900 and to passengers exactly a week later; initially trains ran only as far as Rolvenden, over a mile short of Tenterden, but a new station much closer to the town was opened on 16th March 1903. Anticipating that a number of extensions would be built, the company changed its name to the Kent & East Sussex Railway Company, but in fact despite proposals for extensions south-eastwards from Northiam to Rye, south-eastwards from Tenterden to Appledore, and westwards from Tenterden to Cranbrook, the only extension was north-westwards to Headcorn and this opened on 15th May 1905. At its peak, there were six daily return journeys on weekdays along the full length of the line, although by the early 1950's the level of services had greatly reduced. There were a number of intermediate stations and halts between Robertsbridge and Headcorn; the section of interest to us, between Robertsbridge and Bodiam, boasted not only stations at these locations but two intermediate halts without buildings, Salehurst and Junction Road. Bodiam station, popular for visitors to the nearby castle, did have a building although its design was somewhat rudimentary. The journey time for the four mile ride from Robertsbridge to Bodiam averaged 10 minutes. For many years the line was managed by H.F. Stephens, who also managed the Selsey Tramway described elsewhere in this book. Stephens was noted for his zest for economy and his tendency to swap locomotives between various lines under his control; as on the Selsey Tram, the railway saw the deployment of primitive petrol railbuses in place of steam locomotives. It was Stephens' refusal to allow the line to become incorporated into one of the four new companies during the 1923 amalgamation that meant that the line kept its independence right up until 1948 when it came under the control of British Railways. However, since 1932 the line had become unprofitable and just six years after becoming part of BR the line closed, the final passenger service running on 2nd January 1954, albeit goods services south from Tenterden continued until 1961. A preservation society was subsequently formed and on 3rd February 1974 weekend passenger services were resumed between Tenterden and Rolvenden; gradually the operation extended south-westwards, by 2000 the line was extended to Bodiam, and this Tenterden-Bodiam line, the so-called Kent & East Sussex Railway (KESR), is still at the time of writing an immensely popular tourist attraction. That leaves two separate stretches that remain uncovered by the preserved line. The section from Tenterden to Headcorn is wholly in Kent and is covered in my guide to walking the disused railways of that county. That just leaves the section which is subject of the description below, linking Robertsbridge with Bodiam, all in East Sussex; a short section of line is still in place at Robertsbridge, forming the Rother Valley Railway, and at the other end, just under a mile of track has been laid from Bodiam south-westwards towards Robertsbridge. It is hoped that one day the link between Robertsbridge and Bodiam will be restored, but having regard to the amount of work still to do, that day seems still very far off indeed.

Walking the Line

Exiting Robertsbridge station, proceed to the station car park adjacent to the station building. Here you can view what is now the headquarters of the Rother Valley Railway, and you can inspect the terminus of the old line, some of the rolling stock acquired by the company, and the line itself as it set out on its journey eastwards. It is impossible to follow it, so walk down to Station Road and turn left, following Station Road towards the village centre. Just past the Gray Nicholls buildings on the left, and more or less opposite Willow Bank to the right, turn left along a metalled driveway; it looks rather private but there is a right of way and very shortly it becomes a proper footpath striking out across the fields. Go forward to arrive soon at a bridge under the old line - completely inaccessible here - and proceed along the path beyond, keeping a stream to your right until you reach a footbridge over the stream. Cross the footbridge and bear right; not hard right along the path beside the stream, but next right, heading back to the old line. On reaching the embankment, bear left to walk beside the old line briefly and arriving at a break in the embankment. It may be possible to scramble up onto the embankment just to the right of the break, and walk back towards Robertsbridge, but when you reach the bridge you passed under a few minutes before, you can go no further; the laid section of the Rother Valley railway came up to stop just a little bit short of the bridge on the other side. So return to the break in the embankment and cross to the far (south) side of the old line, following parallel with it and keeping it immediately to the left to arrive at a road, just north of the centre of Robertsbridge. The course of the old line can't realistically be followed or even discerned across the fields immediately east of this road, so turn left and follow the road to the roundabout with the busy A21, carefully crossing straight over and following the minor road towards Salehurst.

It is a pleasant road walk to Salehurst less than a mile away, the course of the old line proceeding parallel with this road to the right and just a short way away, but completely obscured in the fields and it's easier to follow with the eyes than attempt to walk over the fields themselves. Salehurst has two distinguishing features: a church with a splendid and very conspicuous tower, and a pub right on the route, called Salehurst Halt in deference to the railway halt of the same name that stood close by! Just beyond the pub the road bends sharp left, but you keep straight ahead past the church along a bridlepath which soon bends south-eastwards (don't be misled by a wider track which heads off to the right immediately beyond the church; it is a dead end) and descends, crossing the course of the old line, its course hereabouts a great deal clearer but still inaccessible. Go forward along the track to very shortly reach a crossing over the Rother (1) at Church Bridge. Immediately before Church Bridge turn left to follow a crude path along a right-hand field edge parallel with the Rother which is to the right and the course of the old line which is to your left, soon arriving at a crossing of a narrow tributary stream. There is a very narrow plank bridge over this stream which you should cross with care, then continue along the field edge to arrive at an area of woodland. Your thin path enters the woodland, still keeping the course of the old line just to your left and the Rother immediately to your right, and you cross two fences in very close succession using crude stiles.

Beyond the fences, the going then gets a great deal easier and clearer; it's lovely, very easy walking in beautiful surroundings along the left-hand field edge, the Rother meandering away to the right, and the course of the old line very obvious, but not really accessible, to the left. You're forced away from the field edge on reaching a fence, but head alongside the fence towards the river to the right, and a crossing is available, beyond which you simply then return to the field edge to continue beside the old line. Now you see the Rother coming in from the right, and you arrive at the point where

It is hoped to extend the Kent & East Sussex Railway to Robertsbridge from Bodiam thus rendering the walk between these two stations redundant. This is currently as far as the extension goes - a very picturesque sight!

the old line crossed the Rother by means of a bridge. At first sight the bridge crossing seems to be obstructed by barbed wire but walk round to the far side of the bridge and you can scramble up onto it, avoiding the barbed wire, using the metal railings. You should seek permission to cross this bridge and refer to my introductory notes; if there is a problem with crossing the bridge, I set out an alternative in the next paragraph.

If you have crossed the Rother using the bridge, return to the left-hand field edge. There is no path really to speak of and the going is slightly rougher, but keeping the course of the old line (still itself inaccessible) immediately to your left, continue to just short of the Cripps Corner-Hawkurst road where you arrive at a farm track onto which you turn left and which you follow to arrive at the road; this was the site of Junction Road halt. Cross over the road and more or less opposite there's a gated driveway leading to the buildings of Udiam. *If you find the bridge over the Rother obstructed, or you're not happy about crossing it, you'll need to return to the point (1) above, cross Church Bridge and continue southwards to the Robertsbridge Abbey approach road. Turn left here and proceed along the road which beyond the abbey bends round to the right and then bends sharp left, heading in a straight line. A signpost then indicates a bridleway going off to the right and and a footpath straight on; you keep to the footpath, heading straight ahead and now proceeding as signposted in an easterly direction. Keep to the path, using the left-hand field edge, all the way to the Cripps Corner-Hawkhurst road, then turn left to follow the road briefly to a gated driveway on the right, leading to the buildings of Udiam.*

You now follow the gated driveway referred to in the above paragraph; it looks private but there's a plinth sign to reassure you so having gone through the gate you proceed towards the buildings. The old line is just parallel with you to the left but not discernible at all. Look out carefully for, and follow, a signed path leaving the track to the right just before the buildings; the path goes to the right but very quickly swings to the left, just south of east, and climbs steeply to reach a T-junction with a farm lane. Turn left here and, keeping the farm outbuildings to the left, walk up to another T-junction with another - metalled - farm lane. The signed right of way goes to the right, but you need to bear left, shortly veering right and downhill; the lane then veers sharply right again (2), but by going straight on down the bank you'll reach the course of the old line again, and you may be surprised to find that the track has been relaid here. If you look to the left, you'll see the track coming to an end just a short distance away, most picturesquely in woodland just to the north of the Udiam buildings. It really is a lovely spot, and sums up the attractions of the country railway. This is the extent, at the time of writing, of the relaid track from Bodiam back towards Robertsbridge, but whilst it may now seem tempting to simply walk along the newly laid track to Bodiam, DO NOT DO SO. Trains on the Kent & East Sussex Railway may well be using the track so not only will you be trespassing but you will be endangering the safety of the train crew and passengers as well as yourself. However you can stay within sight of the old line virtually all the way to Bodiam. Return to the farm lane at the point (2) above and follow it alongside the old line for roughly half a mile until the lane then swings right (3), uphill, away from the course of the old line. You could now simply follow the lane up to reach a lane junction very shortly; turn left and, looking down on the newly laid track, follow the lane to a road, then turn left downhill to arrive at Bodiam station. As an alternative, it should be possible to enter the field to the left as the lane starts to climb away from point (3) above, and then follow the left-hand field edge round, soon being able to follow beside the course of the old line again. At the far end of the field, bear round to the right and use the gap in the hedge to enter a second field, following the edge of that to arrive within sight of Bodiam station yard where your walk ends. You could take a chance and surmount the gates leading into the yard, but I really can't recommend this course. You'd be better advised to retrace your steps and rejoin the lane at the point (3) above, and walk round to the station via the lane and the road.

If you've planned your walk carefully, you can enjoy refreshment at the station café then pick up a train to Northiam or Tenterden, from each of which there are good bus connections to railheads at Ashford, Hastings and Rye. If you go all the way to Tenterden you could follow the delightful section of old line to Headcorn, described in my Walking The Disused Railways Of Kent. Instead, or as well, you could continue along the road to explore Bodiam's magnificent old castle in superb grounds with a popular tea-room (it is not necessary to pay the castle admission fee to patronise it). If you've chosen a day when trains aren't running, you've a choice. You could retrace your steps to Robertsbridge the same way, or, by way of variation, when you reach the Cripps Corner-Hawkhurst road and the site of Junction Road halt, turn left and then shortly right along a signed footpath. This crosses fields and then soon joins the left bank of the Rother, going forward to a lane which can be followed past Robertsbridge Abbey. Roughly a quarter of a mile beyond the abbey, bear right onto a path which soon reaches Church Bridge, then continue back to Robertsbridge the way you came, via Salehurst. Alternatively, you could decide to walk on to Northiam, 4 miles away. It is a very enjoyable walk, partly on the Sussex Border Path. Turn right out of the station yard and, joining the road, walk uphill to the next road junction, then turn left up Dagg Lane to arrive at a T-junction where you turn left to follow a road into Ewhurst Green. Walk along the lovely main street at Ewhurst Green, going past the church which is to your right, then just beyond the church look out for and follow a signed path downhill along a left-hand field edge with an orchard immediately to your left. Soon you are directed into the orchard, but continue downhill in the same direction, then at the bottom, turn left to follow the right-hand edge of the orchard north-eastwards. At the far north-eastern end, turn right to walk parallel with the road downhill, at length emerging onto the road and following it briefly downhill towards a stream. However, just before the bridge over the stream, turn left onto a path following the right-hand field edge, keeping the stream to your right; you cross the stream and enter another field, walking across it on an obvious path and aiming for another footbridge over the stream which describes an elaborate meander between footbridges! Don't cross this second footbridge but turn right onto a clear path, going south-eastwards and keeping the stream to your left. The obvious path moves a little away from the stream, passing an area of trees and going forward across pasture, crossing a further footbridge over a different stream and then shortly passing over the original stream for the last time. Maintaining your south-easterly direction, you go forward to reach a road just by the house with the picturesque name Strawberry Hole. Cross the road and join the signed path directly opposite; it starts to climb, going forward to follow the left-hand field edge, but you need to drift a little away from it to the right to arrive at a crossroads of paths, aiming for the path that makes the most direct ascent of the steep hill rather than clinging to the left-hand field edge. Look out for and take an unsigned path going off to the right, contouring the hill and aiming for the trees. Keeping to the obvious signed path, you veer very gently left, just north of east, to join a wide gravelled lane and follow it uphill to arrive at Northiam's main street, with the church immediately over the road. There is a bus stop just past the church.

Part of the relaid section of track near Bodiam on the line from Robertsbridge.

WALK 14 - **RYE TO CAMBER SANDS**

WALK 14 - RYE TO CAMBER SANDS

Length:	3 miles.
Start:	Rye.
Finish:	Camber.
Public Transport:	Regular trains serving Rye on the Brighton-Ashford International line; regular buses (SC) serving Camber on the Lydd-Rye-Hastings route.
Refreshments:	Rye (P,S,C); Camber (P,S).
Conditions:	This is a delightful walk. It is extremely easy, the surroundings are very attractive, much of the old line is available for walking, and Rye with its wealth of beautiful buildings and refreshment opportunities makes an ideal base. It will take no more than half a day to complete.

History

This line, at the far south-eastern corner of East Sussex, is always known as the Rye & Camber Tramway; like the Selsey Tramway, the Rye & Camber Tramway was not a true tramway at all, but a light railway which was in fact opened just two years before the Selsey line, in 1895. It did have two other things in common with the Selsey line. Firstly, it linked a place of immense historical interest with a more modest but still bustling seaside community, and secondly it was another of the Colonel Stephens railways, run with an eye to economy, At the time of the opening, on 13th July 1895, it only ran as far as Golf Links Halt adjoining Rye Golf Club and during the first six months of operation of the line, a total of 18,000 tickets were sold for the eight and a half minute journey of a mile and three quarters, with most of the customers being golfers, paying 4d return for the privilege. It is said that golfing passengers had the habit of pulling out the pin between the first two carriages, leaving the passengers in the second carriage stranded! With the extension to Camber Sands, opened exactly 13 years after the opening of the Rye-Golf Links Halt section, the line also became attractive to holidaymakers bound for the superb sands and sandhills around Camber.

There were just three stations on the line. The first of these, Rye, was a completely different station from the one that existed and indeed still exists on the Hastings-Ashford line (the Tramway was wholly separate from that line, with no rail link between the two); the Rye terminus on the Camber line was hardly palatial, but its sturdy corrugated iron structure boasted a waiting room and an office, and there were two sets

Sheep may safely graze…now that this part of the Rye-Camber line is a footpath.

of engine sheds. Next came Golf Links Halt, the single intermediate station, which until the extension to Camber Sands station was described on maps as Camber. It was much more modest, consisting simply of a corrugated iron shed and single platform within sight of the Rye golf clubhouse; one curiosity about the station was that it had a urinal for males wishing to answer the call of nature but Colonel Stephens, a bachelor, made no provision for the ladies! The station building still survives today as a storehouse for the golf club and the exterior looks in very respectable condition. Camber Sands, the eastern terminus, was the most basic of all, with no ticket office - tickets had to be issued by the guard or the driver - nor any shelter for passengers; a photograph of the station in 1938 shows a generous-sized platform and a rather feeble tea-hut. The track ran on for a couple of hundred yards beyond the terminus. At the time of opening, the line had just one locomotive and one carriage, but later two more locomotives were added, one being petrol powered; the tramway also acquired a second carriage and a small quantity of goods wagons for the conveyance of shingle from the nearby beach for ballast.

Traffic began to suffer between the wars as golfers started to make more use of road transport to get to the golf links, but following the outbreak of World War 2 in 1939, the Tramway was abandoned altogether and Camber was evacuated because of invasion fears. The last passenger services ran on 4th September 1939. The line was requisitioned by the Navy in 1943 to link a training establishment set up near Rye station with the harbour, and areas of the track were concreted over for the benefit of road vehicles; the Navy also used the track to transport shingle from the Camber Sands area to supply dumps in the Rye area. Sadly, when the war came to an end, the cost of properly relaying the track proved to be too great and the line never reopened. Rye station was demolished in 1947 but as stated above, Golf Links Halt still survives as do some fragments of the concreted Tramway.

Walking the Line

From the centre of Rye, make your way down to Fishmarket Road which runs below the town to its east, and proceed northwards to the roundabout, turning right here onto the A259 New Road, signposted Folkestone; very soon you cross a bridge over the Rother, and almost immediately beyond the bridge turn right onto a footpath signposted for Camber. This was the site of the old Rye station and terminus of the Tramway. Do not turn hard right here on to the riverside embankment path but follow the signed footpath south-eastwards in a straight line; this is the course of the old line which you can follow by keeping to the footpath all the way to a sizeable lake, and in fact the old line proceeded on in the same direction across land which has now been completely submerged by this lake. You therefore need to bear left, keeping to the footpath, hugging the north shore of the lake and soon arriving at Camber Road. Turn right onto the road and walk beside it (using the path on the left side), continuing to keep the lake immediately to your right; in less than half a mile you reach the south-eastern end of the lake, and just beyond this point you turn right onto a metalled road which is signposted as a private road. Shortly the road swings from southwards to south-eastwards, a footpath coming in from the right at this point (1), and you now find yourself back on the course of the old line with the old tracks still visible. Continue to follow the road south-eastwards, now passing Rye golf course, but take care as the twelfth hole actually crosses this road; the road continues

Some remaining very tangible evidence of the Rye-Camber line.

Two views of the picturesque Rye-Camber line, providing a short but enjoyable walk.

in more or less a straight line and arrives at the green hut which was once Golf Links Halt station. You can see how convenient this would have been for golfers! Continue along the path indicated by the signboard, keeping the fence to your left and soon arriving at a gate; pass through the gate onto a permissive path which swings in a more easterly direction to follow the course of the old line along an embankment. This really is lovely walking with Rye golf course immediately beside you and fine views back to the cliffs around Fairlight just east of Hastings.

The very well signposted path continues, keeping another golf course, the Jubilee course, to your right, and sandhills ahead; following the signposts, you at length arrive at a sturdy shelter with seats - welcome on a wet windy day - and now heads towards the sand dunes, in fact keeping a ridge of sandhills to the left. There is no trace whatsoever of the old Tramway or the Camber Sands terminus which was sited not far beyond the shelter. Now re-enacting what would have been a popular walk for many of the users of the line, continue along the signed path which in fact veers slightly right to cross one of the golf course fairways and go forward to a gate. Pass through it and almost immediately you reach a T-junction with a sandy track. Here you could turn right and walk up a steep hill to enjoy a splendid view to Camber Sands, but in order to reach Camber you need to turn left on arriving at the sandy track; the track arrives at a field which you cross, soon reaching the road and the village of Camber from which there are frequent buses back to Rye. Rather than wait for a bus you could of course return to Rye on foot the way you came - it isn't that far!

WALK 15 - RYE TO RYE HARBOUR

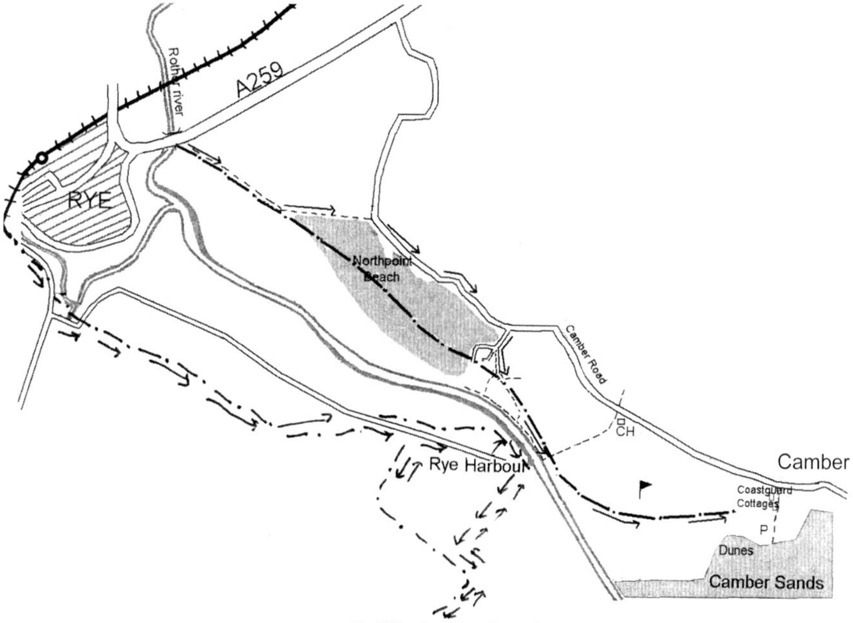

Rother river

A259

RYE

Northpoint Beach

Camber Road

Rye Harbour

CH

Camber

Coastguard Cottages

P

Dunes

Camber Sands

To Winchelsea Beach

WALK 15 - RYE TO RYE HARBOUR

Length:	2 miles minimum, 9.5 miles maximum.
Start:	Rye station.
Finish:	Rye Harbour.
Public Transport:	Regular trains serving Rye on the Brighton-Ashford International line; regular buses (ESCC) from Rye Harbour back to Rye.
Refreshments:	Rye (P,C,S); Rye Harbour (P,C).
Conditions:	Apart from one piece of dull road walking, this is a delightful and interesting walk; it is also very easy and can easily be accomplished in an afternoon, perhaps after a morning spent walking the Rye & Camber Tramway! There is the option of a further railway walk from Rye Harbour which is described below.

History

Rye is an old town and port, but for centuries now it has been set well back from the sea; its port effectively became the separate and nearby village of Rye Harbour, close to the mouth of the Rother estuary. The main line from Hastings to Ashford via Rye opened in 1851, and three years later, in March 1854, a branch to Rye Harbour was added, leaving the main line just south-west of Rye itself. It was a freight-only line, being used to transport flints which had been shipped here from Dungeness, and it also served, via sidings, an oil refinery, concrete works and chemical works. The terminus of the line was in fact a short wooden pier. The line closed in the early 1960's.

Walking the Line

Starting from Rye station, turn right out of the station forecourt onto the A268 Station Approach, veering left to arrive at a junction with Wish Street/Cinque Ports Street. Turn right into Wish Street, going forward to cross the bridge over the river Tillingham and join Winchelsea Road (A259), immediately swinging sharply left. Just beyond this left swing, you could detour right down a lane past buildings on each side; stop when you get to the point where the buildings end and the fields take over, and you'll be standing on the point where the old line crossed, right to left, branching off the extant railway which can be seen across the fields to the right. It can't be followed, though, so having followed its eastward course with the eyes along the edge of the trees to the left, walk back to Winchelsea Road. Follow Winchelsea Road a little further, past a petrol station, then take the first left turning along the road signposted Rye Harbour; you immediately cross the river Brede, adjacent to and immediately to the right of the point at which the old line crossed the river.

Having crossed the river, you'll observe a signed path going off to the right, in fact the Saxon Shore Way bound for Winchelsea. Don't take this path, but swing left with the road and as you do, you'll immediately see another signed path going off to the right, through some thick vegetation, effectively running at right-angles to the Winchelsea-bound path. Take this path, now following the course of the old line, and having emerged from the vegetation you can now follow the obvious course of the old line south-eastwards on a low embankment. Although it isn't marked on OS maps as such, it is indeed a right of way and lovely walking it is as well, with fine views to Camber Castle to the right. You veer slightly right and arrive at a footpath junction, with a signed path going off in a southerly direction, but you need to take the path going to the left, maintaining a south-easterly direction and keeping to the course of the old line. You arrive at a more open sandy area, where the path becomes less well defined, but aim just to the right of a pond ahead, and you'll see the path continuing along the right-hand side of the pond. Continue along the path which passes through trees and emerges to go forward to Harbour Road, the path here veering a little from the course of the old line which is to your right. Turn right to follow Harbour Road, soon reaching the point where the old line crossed this road; you'll see that it's quite impossible to access the course of the old line to the left beyond the crossing, as it runs through strictly private industrial works. Therefore you have to stick to the road for the short distance to Rye Harbour village - the only dull bit of the walk. Pass the church, which is on the right, and continue to the next left turn, Mary Stanford Green, bearing left into that road then at the fork turning right into Coastguard Square; aim for the far right-hand corner, go round the far wall and you'll see a flight of steps up an embankment. You're now back on the course of the old line which you can follow back, north-westwards, towards the big factory complex, and at the top end of the embankment you can bear right onto another embankment which formed a small offshoot of the old line leading to the water's edge. Return to the main embankment, and unable to go back any further towards Rye from here, walk back in a south-easterly direction to the far end of the embankment by the riverside; when you reach the end of the embankment, turn right to walk in front of the William the Conqueror pub to the bottom end of Harbour Road. The bus stop, for buses back to Rye, is a short way up Harbour Road on the left.

However, there is the site of another old railway hereabouts which you may wish to explore before returning to Rye. This is a narrow-gauge line built in 1934 and used in the construction of sea defences along Winchelsea Beach, closing for good when the work finished in 1946. It branched off the Rye-Rye Harbour line just south-east of the point where it crossed Harbour Road, and proceeded as far as Pett Level just south-west of Winchelsea Beach, a small seaside community between the mouth of the Rother

Part of the course of a line that linked Rye Harbour with Pett Level and was used in the construction of sea defences.

beyond Rye Harbour, and Hastings. There is absolutely no trace of it now, but much of its course is quite easy to follow. If you want to do it all, it's a total walk of about 7.5 miles, but you can get a good idea of it with a walk just a third as long, and that is what I recommend below. To cover the "walkable" sections, you first need to walk back along Harbour Road towards the church, but shortly before getting to the church you turn left down a lane which follows the course of the old line and goes forward through a gate; although a sign on the gate proclaims it to be a private road, it is actually a public right of way. The course of the old line is along this right of way but in a little over a quarter of a mile the old line struck out to the south-east (left) of this lane, into what is now Rye Harbour Nature Reserve with its profusion of pools and shingle. You should not enter this area as it is an important conservation area and signs warn you to keep out, so you're forced back to Harbour Road.

Turn right onto Harbour Road and walk to the end where a choice of paths is available: either a clear embankment path striking out south-eastwards parallel with the estuary, or a lane heading to your right (southwards) into a caravan park, keeping a Martello tower immediately to your right. You need to follow the second of these, passing the Martello tower, veering right and then left, aiming for and crossing a bridge over a channel of water. Now continue along the obvious path through the nature reserve, observing a high fence to your right, and in just over a quarter of a mile beyond the bridge, you reach a sharp left turn. The course of the old line comes in from the right here, but while it can be followed with the eyes, you cannot physically follow it back across the conservation area. So veer left to continue along the path, heading south-eastwards along what is the course of the old line, arriving at a T-junction with a track going parallel with the shoreline, which is now very close. Now it's up to you. You could turn right along this track which will take you to Winchelsea Beach about two and a half miles away, but there is no evidence of the old line at all, so although it's a very pleasant walk it isn't going to take your appreciation of disused Sussex railways much further. You may decide to retrace your steps to Rye Harbour from the point you reach the shoreline, but I recommend that, for a bit of variety, you turn left (north-eastwards) along the shoreside track as far as the mouth of the Rother, veering sharply north-westwards alongside the Rother back to Rye Harbour.

Disused railway lines are very popular with cyclists as well as walkers. This is a cyclist near East Grinstead on the course of the old Three Bridges-Groombridge line.

WALK 16 - **FARNHAM TO ASH GREEN**

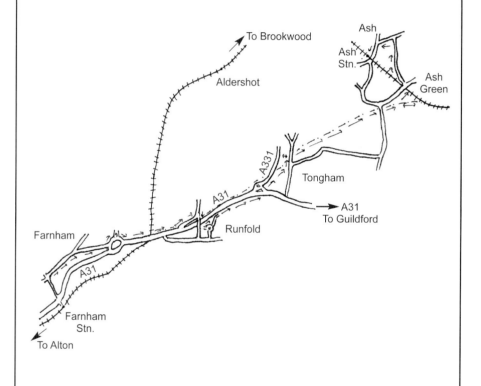

WALK 16 - FARNHAM TO ASH GREEN

Length:	6 miles.
Start:	Farnham (East Street).
Finish:	Ash station.
Public transport:	Regular trains serving Farnham on the Alton-Aldershot-Woking-London Waterloo line; regular buses (SC) serving Farnham from Guildford, Aldershot and Haslemere; regular trains serving Ash on the Guildford-Aldershot-Ascot route.
Refreshments:	Farnham (P,C,S); Runfold (C); Tongham (S).
Conditions:	This is a walk of two halves. The first half has a distinctly urban feel, with traffic noise never far away, but the second half is delightfully rural and very rewarding. You will only require half a day to complete it.

History

Anyone wishing nowadays to travel by train between the two pleasant Surrey towns of Farnham and Guildford will need to go from Farnham to Aldershot and then join a train heading initially north-eastwards, away from Guildford, before veering south-eastwards via Ash. However there was previously a more direct line linking Farnham with Guildford; the area was a well-known barley growing district, and when this line opened in 1849 a considerable amount of traffic of locally-brewed ale was anticipated. Branching off from the extant line at Junction Bridge between Farnham and Aldershot, the old line took a more direct course towards Guildford via Tongham, being reunited with the extant line near Ash Green just east of Ash, and with intermediate stations at Tongham and Ash Green. In 1922 there were 10 or 11 journeys each way Monday-Saturday, with no service on Sunday, and a journey time of around 23 minutes between Farnham and Guildford. The line remained open for nearly 90 years, but when electrification came in 1937, a decision was taken to close this direct line to passenger traffic, meaning that to travel from Farnham to Guildford meant a journey via Aldershot.

Walking the Line

Your walk starts in the centre of the attractive town of Farnham. Follow East Street away from the town centre and then fork right onto the A325 Guildford Road rather

than going straight on along the B3007 Hale Road. When Guildford Road arrives at the Shepherd & Flock Roundabout, bear left and, following the cycle/pedestrian way, keep to the left up the hill beside the main road (A31). As the A31 bends round to the right, you follow it round to the right as well, crossing the arms of the A325 with great care and proceeding parallel with the A31 as signed towards Guildford, continuing to use the cycle/pedestrian way provided as long as it lasts. Stay parallel with the A31 and to the left of it, and cross a bridge over the railway; this is known as Junction Bridge, for it was just here that the old line left the

Although much of the Farnham-Ash Green line cannot be walked, the section between Tongham and Ash Green has been restored for use by walkers.

extant one. Keep walking along the left side of the A31, which unfortunately beyond the bridge is now pavement-less, so take great care, then take the next slip road away from the A31, rising to a junction, with St Georges Road going off to the left (north) and a bridge over the A31 (1) to the right. Bear right as if to cross the bridge, but rather than join the bridge immediately, look down to your right and you can see the course of the old line below you; it's followable with the eyes back to the start of the slip road, and indeed by heading north up St Georges Road briefly and then turning right onto a signed path you can view the embankment of the old line immediately to your right. Walk back to the bridge over the A31 referred to at (1) above and now go onto it.

Now you have a choice. The old line followed the left-hand edge of the A31 as you look north-eastwards along the A31 towards Guildford and indeed you could backtrack to the start of the slip road and walk north-eastwards along the verge of the A31 until you reach and join the A331 exit sliproad; the old line is in fact just parallel with you to the left down the sliproad, but lost in the tangle of vegetation and concrete on the left. On reaching the roundabout at the bottom, cross the A331 with immense care, and just beyond the crossing there's a signed footpath/cycleway going off to the left (2), away from the roundabout, which you need to take to continue your walk. However, the A31 is an extremely busy road and although you are effectively following the course of the old line as closely as you can, it is hardly an enjoyable experience. I therefore recommend that you content yourself with following the course of the old line with your eyes from the bridge indicated at (1) above, but then cross to the other side, and turn almost immediately left down a flight of steps to begin a much safer and pleasanter walk to point (2) above. At the foot of the steps turn right onto a metalled road, very shortly reaching a mini-roundabout on the edge of the village of Runfold, and taking the first exit to the left. This takes you past a complex specialising in vintage interiors - it's a fascinating place, and better still, there's a café - and then on past farm buildings to reach what is a dead end for cars, but beyond which there is a metalled cycle path. Follow this alongside the A31, veering round to pass underneath this road and cross slip roads leading from/to the A31; both are busy, so take care. You then arrive at the signed footpath/cycleway referred to at (2) above, going off to your right.

Follow this path which goes forward into Grange Road and arrives in the outskirts of Tongham. Just before the road bends right to reach the main village street, turn left to follow Garbetts Way and immediately beyond Maitlands Close turn left down a lane towards a gate. You're now on the course of the old line and, beyond an information board which is to your right, you can continue straight on along a newly constructed path following what was the railway line. It is very pleasant walking, with attractive woodland, a new community facility, to your right. Sadly the traffic noise builds up and you reach a dead end just short of the busy A331 road, so retrace your steps to Garbetts Way, but this time turn left and then immediately right along an alleyway beside the backs of houses on the north-western side of Chester Way, following immediately beside the course of the old line. The alleyway arrives at some garages, and you then need to turn left to walk between the garages, veering right immediately beyond them onto a little green; follow the green forward to reach the main street at Tongham. You could detour right to visit the centre of the village, but to continue your walk cross straight over onto a narrow stony path which proceeds along the course of the old line between houses. The path rises and veers slightly right to meet a junction with another path, and where it does, you need to turn left and immediately you will see, to the right, the course of the old line stretching ahead of you heading north-eastwards.

Simply now follow the course of the old line along an excellent path for about a mile. The suburban feel is left behind and the surroundings become extremely pleasant. All too soon, however, you reach two overbridges in close succession, Ash Green station being situated immediately beyond the first, and the second (blue) one marking your point of exit from the line. Immediately before this second overbridge you need to turn right up a steep path (3) leading away from the line. However you can continue along the old line for another few hundred yards, to just short of its junction with the extant Guildford-Aldershot line, and enjoy what is a very pleasant walk, particularly just at the end where the path is in the shade of trees with a steep cutting to the left. You reach a wire fence beyond which you can go no further, so retrace your steps to the steep path at (3) and climb up to reach a lane. Bear left to cross over the old line using the overbridge, then beyond the bridge turn immediately right onto a byway which proceeds pleasantly to a road junction. Turn right onto the road, straightaway crossing the Guildford-Aldershot line, then at the T-junction beyond turn left onto Harper's Road. Follow this road which soon bends right and proceeds past some woodland which is to the left; beyond the woodland there's a short climb and at the top of the climb, there are signed footpaths to the right and left. Turn left here and follow the footpath to arrive at the A323 at Ash, from which it's a short walk along this road to your left to arrive at Ash station.

Old stations are often turned into dwellings; good examples are Cocking (above) on the Chichester-Midhurst line, and Mayfield (below) on the Redgate Mill Junction-Polegate line.

WALK 17 - **BROOKWOOD NECROPOLIS RAILWAY**

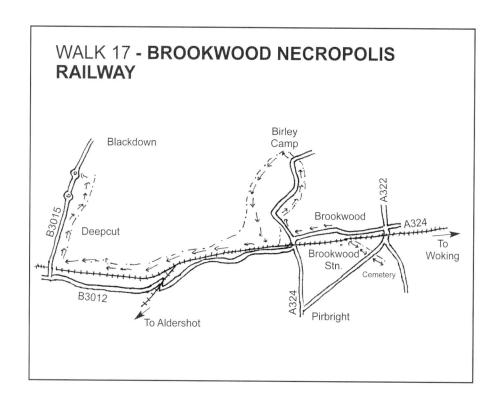

One of many ornate constructions beside the Brookwood Necropolis Railway.

WALK 17 - BROOKWOOD NECROPOLIS RAILWAY

Length:	0.75 miles each way - total 1.5 miles.
Start and finish:	Brookwood station.
Public transport:	Regular trains serving Brookwood on the London Waterloo-Alton and Basingstoke/Southampton lines.
Refreshments:	Brookwood (P,S).
Conditions:	A very short and easy but extremely rewarding walk, which shouldn't take more than 45 minutes there and back and could perhaps be coupled with the Brookwood-Blackdown walk described below to make a long half day's railway exploration.

History

It is thought to be the cholera epidemic of 1848/49 that caused Brookwood Cemetery to be built. Not long afterwards the London & South Western Railway (LSWR) agreed to requests from both locals and the London Necropolis Company for a station on the main London to Southampton line to be provided adjacent to the cemetery, to facilitate the bulk conveyance of coffins there from London. The station, known today as Brookwood, was duly built. Upon arriving at the station, the special trains bearing the coffins and mourners - the coffins conveyed in special hearse vans while the mourners were accommodated in ordinary carriages - were backed into a siding that was created for the purpose, and which became known as the Brookwood Necropolis Railway, opening in 1854 and actually running through the cemetery. Two stations were built on the siding, North and South, with South marking the terminus three quarters of a mile from the main line, and there was also a special private terminus in London where the trains began their sad journeys. The siding at Brookwood remained operational until World War 2 when the London terminus and Necropolis train itself suffered severe bomb damage, and with motor hearses taking the place of the train service, it was decided not to recommence trains into the cemetery after the war. The track was lifted in 1953 and both the North and South stations have since been demolished, although the embankment is clearly visible in places, as is the platform of the South station.

Walking the Line

Using the subway, leave Brookwood station on the down platform side, and turn immediately left onto a clear track which soon bends right and arrives at a crossroads junction with Long Avenue, a chapel straight ahead. Turn left and go up Long Avenue

The terminus of the Brookwood Necropolis Railway.

to its junction with Railway Avenue. It is possible to turn left here (1) and follow what is the course of the old line back towards Brookwood station, but your way forward is in due course blocked so retrace your steps to (1) above and this time continue along Railway Avenue - still on the course of the old line - as far as a road crossing, having to step round a white barrier as you approach the road. Cross the road and turn right then immediately left, following the signs for St Edward Orthodox. Very soon on the left is a sign for the Ismaili Cemetery and close by, a very large tree. Walk between the tree and the modern red brick buildings you can see half left, and you will arrive at the course of the old line, marked by a slightly raised line of trees; as you proceed along what is an obvious course, the embankment becomes wider and clearer. Despite the inevitably sad and sombre associations, the cemetery is very peaceful and beautifully kept. You arrive at a crossing track where you bear right then immediately left through a gap in a little hedge, passing to the left of the twin chapels of St Edward Orthodox and then St Edward Brotherhood, still following the course of the old line; there is a monastic community at St Edward Brotherhood and you may be greeted by the monks as you pass. In front of St Edward Brotherhood, a very striking black and white building, you can clearly see the old South station platform. To return to Brookwood station, you just need to retrace your steps, but you may well wish to linger in the cemetery and explore some of its more unusual features, noting in particular the variety of faiths and denominations represented, before completing your walk.

Looking back to the beautiful St Edward Brotherhood from the terminus of the Brookwood Necropolis Railway.

WALK 18 - **BROOKWOOD TO BLACKDOWN**

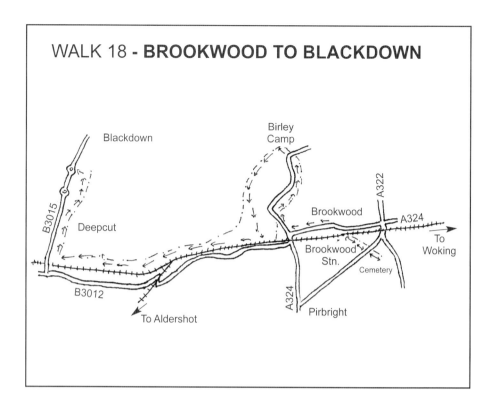

Picturesque woodland on the Brookwood-Blackdown line between Bisley and Pirbright.

WALK 18 - **BROOKWOOD TO BLACKDOWN**

Length:	6 miles.
Start:	Brookwood station.
Finish:	Deepcut village.
Public transport:	Trains to and from Brookwood as per Brookwood Necropolis Railway above; regular buses (CL) linking Deepcut with Brookwood.
Refreshments:	Brookwood (P,S,C); Deepcut (P,S,C).
Conditions:	This is a most interesting and rewarding walk, with only limited walking available on the old line but there is some attractive scenery and one or two real surprises.

History

Initially this railway line ran just as far as Bisley. Opening on 12th July 1890, it was built in order to provide a link between the main London-Southampton railway and the National Rifle Association (NRA) headquarters, which had transferred to Bisley from south London. When World War 1 broke out, the NRA placed its facilities at the disposal of the War Office and large numbers of troops underwent training there, bringing a great deal more custom to the railway line. Moreover, opportunity was taken to extend the line to the nearby army camps at Pirbright, Deepcut and Blackdown, the extension being completed in March 1917, with stations provided at all three camps besides Bisley. The extension was abandoned in the 1920's but the original line to Bisley remained in use, and in 1939 at the outbreak of World War 2 Bisley came into its own again as a centre for small arms training and research. Ironically, after the closure of the original extension (the track actually being lifted) an extension to reach the outskirts of Pirbright was opened in 1941, closing soon after the war. Finally, the line to Bisley itself closed in early 1952, although, as will be seen below, some pieces of evidence of the old line still remain, and the NRA continues on the site.

Walking the Line

Leave Brookwood station by the "up" platform exit - if you've just walked the Necropolis Railway, simply follow the subway from one end to the other - and turn left onto the main street. Follow it to its end, then as the road bends to the left just before the railway bridge, turn right at the junction and cross over the Basingstoke Canal. The old line branched off the existing one just beyond the railway bridge here, and by walking briefly

A tiny piece of surviving railway on the Brookwood-Blackdown line, close to the site of Bisley station.

westwards along the towpath on the left bank of the canal you can observe parts of the abutments of the bridge carrying the old line over the canal, the old line then proceeding northwards through thick woods on the north side of the canal. It can't be followed, though, so return to the road bridge crossing and, having crossed the canal by the road, keep walking up the road, the course of the old line going parallel with this road in the woods. As the road bends sharp left, bear right into Queens Road (with signpost for the NRA) and follow it, the old line parallel with you to your right, down a cutting. It is followable initially, after a scramble down the cutting, but is blocked by a river so you'll need to return to Queens Road and follow it, past the main entrance to the NRA headquarters, as far as the right-hand bend immediately beyond. At the bend, just by the "national speed limit applies" road sign, turn left onto a footpath, now back on the course of the old line. Follow the path to its end, bearing right into a caravan park - one of many on the NRA site - and walking along the left-hand edge of the park to a prominent green corrugated iron building to the left. Immediately beyond this building, turn left up a metalled drive, Marjorie Foster Way, keeping the course of the old line parallel with you and directly to your left. Just before the top end of this drive, there's an amazing surprise: to the left is a little fragment of old railway, a platform, an old railway carriage and the old Bisley Camp station which has been redeveloped into the Lloyds TSB Rifle Club! This was the terminus of the old line for much of its life.

Continue on in a straight line over the crossing driveway, along a pathway which passes to the right of an armoury and proceeds very pleasantly onwards, following the course of the old line. It bends to the left (south-westwards) and crosses Elcho Road, then continues as a path, following the left-hand edge of another caravan park and going forward as an obvious path through the trees, still on the course of the line. The path peters out in an area of trees but you continue in the same direction through the trees, aiming for a high perimeter fence, and here you're forced to lose the old line, which you won't be able to pick up again until the other side of Pirbright Camp. Turn left to follow the perimeter fence all the way round, arriving at Beech Grove, bearing right into this road and following it to a T-junction with Brunswick Road. It's impossible to turn right here, as this is the entrance to Pirbright Camp, access to which is prohibited to unauthorised persons, so turn left at the T-junction along Brunswick Road. Shortly, just beyond the right turn to Peatmore Drive, Brunswick Road veers sharply right, and drops down; as it straightens out at the bottom of the little hill, look carefully out for and turn right onto a path which goes over the Basingstoke Canal. If you were pushed for time you could turn left here and would be back in Brookwood in a few minutes, but to continue towards Deepcut turn right to follow the towpath along the left bank. This is lovely walking; disused railway walking it isn't, but it's a fine interlude in your travels. Continue along the towpath, in one mile reaching the next road bridge crossing (1), actually another part of Brunswick Road, easily recognisable by the steep rise required to reach it and the forbidding locked iron gate to your right on the other side! Walk on along the towpath, which bends decisively left, and in about half a mile from the crossing referred to at (1) above you reach a lock which incorporates a bridge crossing with a beautiful, one might say idyllic, yellow-painted cottage just beyond it on the right. Cross the canal here and very soon reach a fork of tracks, turning right here and walking uphill to reach a junction with another track, turning very hard left - a hairpin bend, if you like - onto this track. You're back on the course of the old line: it can be followed briefly the other way, but shortly at a road junction it strikes out to the south-east and becomes impossible to continue further back to Pirbright Camp, so follow it now in a westerly direction towards Deepcut. The track soon bends to the right and goes uphill, veering away from the course of the old line which you now keep to the left (a barn and recycling station have been built on its course), then dropping gently back down to rejoin the course of the old line again. You continue along the track keeping army buildings to your right (protected by secure fencing), and about 100 yards or so beyond the buildings, look carefully to your right and you'll see a small gully developing to your right with a little embankment behind it. That embankment shortly goes away to the right, and as it does so look out for a very distinctive tree immediately to your left, with a large number of barks. Just opposite this tree, on the right, is another clear embankment, veering off to the right and away from your path. This is the course of the old line, and you may now follow it; it isn't always easy to walk along it, but it is perfectly possible to do so, until you reach a patch of thick vegetation when you need to turn left down the bank, and walk alongside the bottom of the bank for the short distance to your old friend Brunswick Road. This junction marks the site of Deepcut station.

Cross straight over the road and, continuing in the same direction, walk along the right-hand edge of a pleasant green, keeping the Blackdown Barracks and Princess Royal Barracks to your right. Your way ahead seems to be barred by fencing, but at the top corner of the green you'll see there is a grassy path alongside the fence, and you follow this, keeping the course of the old line immediately beside you to your right. You pass immediately to the right of a church and churchyard and keep walking, until you arrive at the far left corner of the fencing; here turn right and very soon you can turn left to follow the clear course of the old line, set apart from the countryside around it by a slightly raised embankment. Soon the vegetation becomes impenetrable, so leave the embankment by turning left and joining a rough path which continues parallel with the course of the old line to reach The Royal Way. Turn right very briefly onto this road, but then take the path going almost immediately left and follow it through the trees to arrive at a T-junction of paths. Bear left here and follow this path through very charming woodland, the course of the old line parallel with you to the left but impossible to follow. In due course you reach another T-junction of paths; turn left to cross the course of the old line, which can't be followed more than a few yards in each direction, and climb up to reach Newfoundland Road. Bear right to follow this road, passing a school which is to your right (actually built on the course of the old line) and arriving at a T-junction with Alma Gardens. Turn right and then very shortly left, making your way between the houses on the course of the old line, to reach another road junction (2) and an open grassy area immediately beyond. This was the terminus of the old line, at Blackdown station, but there is now no trace of it at all.

It now just remains for you to find a bus back to the nearest railhead. Retrace your steps to Alma Gardens and turn right, then left into Cyprus Road where you should be able to pick up a bus to Brookwood and Woking. Alternatively, walk to the end of Cyprus Road, turn right into Newfoundland Road and follow it to its junction with Deepcut Bridge Road (B3015). Turn left here and walk downhill to the centre of Deepcut village with its shop and café, and bus services to Brookwood and Woking.

WALK 19 - CROYDON, MERSTHAM AND GODSTONE IRON RAILWAY

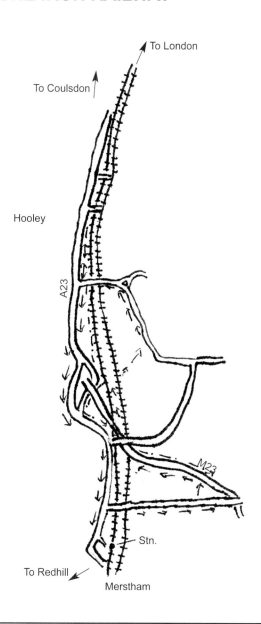

WALK 19 - CROYDON, MERSTHAM AND GODSTONE IRON RAILWAY

Length:	8 miles.
Start and finish:	Merstham station.
Public Transport:	Regular trains serving Merstham on the Redhill-London line.
Refreshments:	Merstham (P,C,S); Hooley (P,C,S).
Conditions:	This is an unusual old railway walk; as very little of the old line can actually be followed, I have created what is a circular walk, and at various points in your circle you will encounter little fragments of evidence of the part of the old line that went through Surrey as it is now. Despite the fact that the amount of old line that's followable is small, there is much of interest for the railway historian and indeed historian generally, there are plenty of refreshment opportunities, it is very scenic in places, and although the walk seems to be dominated by the noise of traffic, it is well worth undertaking. About half a day is needed to complete it.

History

This was one of the first railways ever to be built. July 1803 saw the opening of the world's first public railway, the Surrey Iron Railway linking Wandsworth with Croydon, and the aim of the Croydon, Merstham and Godstone railway was to effectively extend the Surrey Iron Railway to the North Downs, and specifically the lime quarries at Merstham. An extension to Godstone was planned, and also a branch to Reigate, but the line never got further than the Greystone Lime Works half a mile north of Merstham station. In 1838 the line was sold to the London, Brighton & South Coast Railway and that company duly opened its main line from London to Brighton; effectively the old railway became redundant, much of the Surrey part of the route being destroyed by deep cuttings on the approach to the extant Merstham Tunnel. Almost all traces of the old line have been destroyed not only by the existing railway line, but also the M23, and as intimated above, those little pieces of evidence that remain are quite hard to find.

Walking the Line

Leave Merstham station by the main exit, and turn half-right to follow the northern station approach road as far as the T-junction with the main village street. Turn right and follow it, crossing the M25, then turn right into Rockshaw Road; follow the road, crossing the twin railway bridges, and in just over half a mile turn left at the North Downs Way signpost to follow the North Downs Way downhill on a clear stony path. The path veers slightly left to arrive at a bridge carrying the M23, which you go under, then follow the path - still the North Downs Way - as it veers to the right. The path soon straightens and begins to climb gently; as it does, just before you get level with a ruined barn situated much further up the hillside, turn left along a thin path up the bank, reaching a fence at the top. Bear right until you reach a gap in the fence, pass through the gap and immediately turn left to follow alongside the fence, continuing along the left-hand field edge until you're back beside the motorway again. The old line started and finished at the works that were situated hereabouts, and then followed a course immediately beside the motorway heading just north of west. Although this isn't a designated right of way (see my introductory notes), you could do the same, walking through the field and forward into a second field, but in due course you'll reach an area of thick vegetation where further progress will become impossible, so retrace your steps all the way back to the North Downs Way bridge under the motorway. However this time don't veer left back up to Rockshaw Road but turn right onto a signed bridleway, now parallel with the M23 which is immediately to your right.

Proceed initially along the flat, on what is an excellent path in the shade of trees, then rise steadily with the path and at the end you reach a T-junction with the B2031. Cross the B2031 and turn right to follow it, crossing the M23. Immediately beyond the crossing there's a gated private lane going off to the right; there's another gate at the end with a sign prohibiting forward access, and this is on the course of the old line, close to the thick vegetation which will have frustrated progress going the other way. The old line isn't followable north-west of here, as the M23 covers its course, so having inspected the gated private lane, cross straight back over the B2031 and join a signed path directly on the opposite side of the road. Follow it very pleasantly uphill, initially through woodland then emerging into fields; you walk along a right-hand field edge, then veer gently right and follow a clear path across the middle of the field to arrive at a road, Dean Lane. Turn left and follow this road downhill to arrive at a junction with the A23. Just before you reach the junction you'll see a useful roadside café, and if you look closely between the near side end of the café by Dean Lane and the lane itself, you'll see an old brick bridge which carried the old line under Dean Lane. The café can therefore be seen to have been built right over the old line! Pass the café then turn right to follow beside the A23 (there is thankfully a pavement), the course of the old line running immediately to your right as you continue, then in half a mile or so you'll arrive at a set of traffic lights at the village of Hooley, which is on the opposite side of the A23. Here turn right into Forge Bridge Road and immediately you'll see a remarkable sight: the two extant London-Brighton railway lines, one "slow" and one "fast" line, the latter avoiding Merstham and Redhill) separated by a tall green embankment. It is a magnificent piece of railway engineering but it has destroyed all traces of the old line.

You could, if you wished, return to the A23 and, keeping the course of the old line immediately to your left, walk on up for another half mile to the signed border between Surrey and the Greater London Borough of Croydon, where the old line crossed the A23. But as there is nothing of the old line to see, I really don't recommend it!

This is the far end of the circular walk, so now you need to head back towards Merstham, retracing your steps down the A23 to the café and continuing past it along the parallel slip road. The course of the old line is through the gardens of the houses to your left, and ahead of you is a rather intricate junction. If you wanted to stay as faithful to the course of the old line as possible, you'd need to keep walking on the left side of the A23, ignoring the signed walkers' crossing (1) with signpost advising that Merstham is a mile and a half away, and then, when the slip road down to the motorway goes off to the left, cross the slipway to join a cycle path adjoining the southbound carriageway of the A23. You soon veer right to pass under a motorway overbridge, then veer left beside the road, the course of the old line lost in the trees to your left, and to your relief, can go forward to reach a pavement. However until you reach the sanctuary of the pavement, this is actually quite a dangerous option, as the cycle path doesn't extend all the way along it, the traffic can be heavy, and the crossing of the motorway slip road isn't a pleasant undertaking either! You may accordingly prefer the safer route below which while less faithful to the course of the old line makes a more agreeable walk. Cross the road at the point (1) above, then bear left to simply walk beside the road - the northbound carriageway of the A23 - keeping the road to your left; there's pavement throughout, so you're in no danger from the traffic. You pass the point where the slip road off the M23 comes down to join the A23, and reach a point where the pavement on your side ends and there's a crossing to a continuation of the pavement on the other side. You're now reunited with the more direct but more dangerous route described above.

As you continue on towards Merstham, veering south-eastwards beside what are now two adjacent carriageways of the A23, look down to your left, and there you'll see a wooded cutting bearing the course of the old line, with which you can walk parallel while it lasts. At length it ends, and the course of the old line is now lost, this time for good, as you near the M23 again. Continue on past the B2031 left turn; by walking up the B2031 over the motorway bridge you'd find the gated private lane you'll have seen earlier on. Beyond the B2031 turning you go past an Indian restaurant, formerly a pub, and, passing Merstham church which is to the right, you soon arrive at the Rockshaw Road junction which is to your left. Simply then retrace your steps to Merstham, crossing the M25. If you're anxious to get on your way, turn first left beyond the M25 underbridge to follow Station Road North down to the station, but if you've time in hand, follow the main road a little further and turn right to enjoy Merstham's undoubted architectural highlight, Quality Street. This is a beautiful lane full of lovely old houses. Having strolled up and down the street, there are plenty of places to get some refreshment before catching the train home.

WALK 20 - EWELL WEST TO WEST PARK HOSPITAL (HORTON LIGHT RAILWAY)

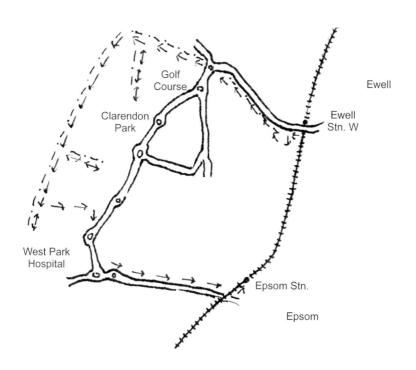

WALK 20 - EWELL WEST TO WEST PARK HOSPITAL (HORTON LIGHT RAILWAY)

Length:	4 miles excluding detours; add 2 miles for both detours and up to 1.5 miles more if it's necessary to walk back to Epsom.
Start:	Ewell West station.
Finish:	Clarendon Park estate.
Public Transport:	Regular and very frequent trains serving both Ewell West and Epsom on the London-Epsom/Dorking/Horsham line; regular buses (EPS) between Clarendon Park and Epsom.
Refreshments:	Epsom (P,C,S).
Conditions:	After a slow start, this really is a delightful walk, in mostly very attractive surroundings, ideal for a half-day ramble and good for families (with the incentive, for children, of a working farm visit at the end). It works very well as a continuous route, but there are two possible detours if you have the time and inclination and want to maximise your old railway exploration.

History

This was actually not just one line but a mini-network of contractors' lines that were installed to assist the construction of the so-called Horton group of hospitals for the mentally handicapped, and which supplied the hospitals with coal and other goods. The hospitals, marked as "asylums" on earlier maps of the area, were situated just to the north-west of Epsom, and the mini-network consisted of a principal line branching off the main Southern network near Ewell West (on the Dorking-London Waterloo line) and ending at the asylum just off the Epsom-Oxshott road, with two branches, one serving the so-called Long Grove hospital and the other supplying a hospital boiler house with coal. The line opened in 1913 and closed in 1950. Two of the "asylums" were subsequently closed, one being turned into a housing development and one into a traditional hospital, and the grounds in which they were built became part of Horton Country Park, now a very fine leisure facility including a popular golf course. Better still for walkers, much of the course of the old line and its branches were converted into public footpaths, and the result is some of the nicest and most rewarding railway walking in Surrey. Interestingly one of the paths through the park is known as Hendon Grove, named after one of the locomotives used to operate the light railway.

Walking the Line

Your walk starts at Ewell West station. Make your way from the station exit onto Chessington Road, and stand on the bridge carrying this road over the railway, immediately south of the station; looking southwards towards Epsom, the old line branched off to the right very shortly south of the bridge. However, there is no trace of the join, and, thanks to modern development, no trace of the old line hereabouts, and there really is no point in wandering along the various side roads to see the course the old line would have taken, so head westwards along Chessington Road, away from the centre of Ewell, beyond the bridge. Turn shortly left into Longmead Road then first right into Hollymoor Lane and second left into Somerset Close; at the bottom of Somerset Close you hit the course of the old line which has come up from the extant Epsom-Ewell line (the map shows it branching off south-westwards from the extant line, then striking out north-westwards to reach this point). Turn right at the bottom of Somerset Close into Lincoln Walk, veering right to arrive back at Hollymoor Lane, following roughly the course of the old line as you do so, then turn briefly left onto Hollymoor Lane and very shortly right into Melton Place, going forward into Melton Fields. As you progress along Melton Fields you pass a parking area for local residents which is on the left, and at the top end of this parking area is an alleyway onto which you turn left and which approximately follows the course of the old line (its course to the right of Melton Fields is impossible to follow). In a few yards you reach a T-junction with a footpath, a green area immediately beyond; more or less opposite this T-junction is a gate, and you pass through the gate to enter this green area.

Now the walk becomes much more interesting and enjoyable. Proceed across the green area in a north-westerly direction, following the same line as the alleyway referred to immediately above; the course of the old line can clearly be identified to the right, through the tufty grass that separates the green area from the line of housing behind Chessington Road which is running parallel with you to your right. Once or twice it's possible to walk into the tufty grass and see the course of the old line in a little dip between the green area and the back gardens. It's not practicable to walk along it, though, so stick to the comfort of the green area; it's a very popular place for people to walk their dogs, so don't expect to be alone! There are two or three strips of vegetation across the green area which appear to interrupt progress, but there are clear paths through them, so just keep going, aiming for the far end of the green area at a point just to the south-west (left) of a roundabout junction of Chessington Road (B2200) and the B284 Hook Road. The course of the old line, impossible to follow hereabouts, remains parallel with you to your right. Exit the green area and cross straight over the B284 Hook Road, going forward to enter the approach road and car park for the Horton Park Golf & Country Club; as you reach the car park, bear sharply right and go ahead to view the only surviving piece of railway engineering of this old line, namely the brick parapets of an old overbridge. They look rather incongruous now but each parapet proudly bears a plaque with a reminder of the railway and its operating dates. Having

Two views of the very attractive walk through Horton Country Park following lines built to service the hospitals in the area.

inspected the parapets, make your way across the car park to the golf clubhouse, and proceed past the golf shop, emerging on the golf course side of the clubhouse and going forward to what is marked as a "cleaning area" on the left; turn right here onto a path and follow it, soon reaching a path junction, bearing left here and following a path to what is the 10th tee of the golf course. As you reach it, bear right to walk round the near side of it, and you'll find yourself at an embankment - the course of the old line -

and looking back, you should be able to see the course of the line from the parapets. Now walk along the left side of the embankment, soon reaching a break in it, with a gate, and it's at this point that you can see, and now join, a clear path going ahead of you along the course of the old line.

It is lovely to be on the old line "proper" and delightful walking it is too, in the shade of woodland which is cool and refreshing in summer. Initially you proceed in a dead straight line, but within sight of a gentle but obvious bend to the left, there is a junction (1) with a clear path going off to the left, being a branch line going off to Long Grove Hospital. It is possible to take a detour along this branch (the out-and-back walk will take about 10/15 minutes each way). The description of the main route continues below, but your detour is as follows. Begin by proceeding very pleasantly through woodland as far as a T-junction. Turn left here, soon being joined by another path coming in from the right, and veer gently right to proceed in a southerly direction with the golf course both to your right and to your left, following the course of the old line. In a few hundred yards you reach a major path junction with wide paths forking both right and left. The course of the old line, straight ahead, is completely lost in thick vegetation, but by following the right fork (2) briefly you can see the course the old line would have taken, ending in what was Long Grove Hospital but which is now the Clarendon Park housing estate, and you can see the houses at the north end of the estate from your path. You have the option here of a short cut, saving about a mile of walking (see italicised section below); otherwise retrace your steps, remembering to take the right fork at the top end of the golf course, and then turning very shortly right again, soon arriving back at the junction at (1) above and bearing left to continue on the main route.

Whether or not you've made the detour above, continue now along the main route that, as intimated above, bends gently to the left and heads south-westwards. About half a mile from the first detour, you arrive at a meeting of your path with the Chessington Countryside Walk, signed off your path to the right and to the left. However, you need to continue along the main path south-westwards, still on the course of the old line, and shortly on the left-hand side is a junction (3) with a path going off to the left, which is a second branch off the main line and provides a possibility of another, somewhat shorter detour (no more than 5-10 minutes each way). If you decide to make the detour, simply follow the path which soon arrives at a T-junction (4) with a path (5), one of the main paths serving the country park but not following an old railway line! Directly ahead is a field, with a hedge bordering the right-hand side of it; the old line proceeded over what is now the near part of the field, crossing over into the adjacent field to the right. To view that, turn right onto the path (5) above and shortly you can look left to see the course of the old line heading across the field, bound for the old hospital boiler house. You can now appreciate the reason for this branch, which was to supply the boiler house with coal, and the old boiler house is still a prominent feature today as part of a smart new leisure centre. However there's no right of way into either field and there is little to be gained by proceeding - following the course of the old line with the eyes will suffice - so retrace your steps back to the main path at the junction at (3) above, and turn left.

It is possible to make a link between the ends of both detours described above to create a continuous walk and save you about a mile of walking, although it will mean missing out on about half a mile of the "main railway" path. To do this, don't retrace your steps at the end of the first detour but continue along the right fork referred to at (2) above, the Chessington Countryside Walk soon coming in hard from the right. Don't bear right here, and ignore the path going off to the left here too, but keep going until you shortly reach another path coming in from the right; this is the junction referred to at (4) above and is the bottom end of the second detour. Turn right to follow the path back to the "main railway" path, and turn left.

Back on the main path, you now follow it on, proceeding past a delightful pond, continuing to what looks like a T-junction and the end of this main path (6). I recommend you go straight over onto what is a very thin path carrying straight on beyond this junction; this thin path follows the course of the old line taking you to the extant hospital, and the end of the principal line on this network. However, this is a dead end, so having got, literally, to the end of the line, retrace your steps to (6) above and turn right, in due course arriving at another T-junction of paths. Turn right here, and follow a clear path, passing a picnic area which is to your left and arriving at a road (7), Horton Lane, with Epsom accessible on foot by turning right here. However, on Mondays to Saturdays there are buses from the Clarendon Park estate back to Epsom, and en route to the estate you could get a closer view of the boiler house and also visit the Horton Park Children's Farm which is a lovely family attraction. To access all these, turn left onto Horton Lane and simply follow it, soon crossing a mini-roundabout and almost immediately beyond, reaching left turnings to the boiler house and the farm, with clearly signed detours to each. The boiler house (as stated above, part of a leisure centre) is a particularly impressive structure, and you can look beyond it to see the course the old line would have taken to reach it from the end of the second detour described above, although it is definitely not accessible. Beyond the turnings off Horton Lane to the boiler house and the farm you soon reach another roundabout, now having reached the Clarendon Park estate which is accessible to the left via McKenzie Way; accordingly, turn left here into McKenzie Way, with very conspicuous bus stops and at the time of writing a frequent regular service to Epsom.

Even if buses aren't running from here, you may of course wish to detour to the boiler house and the farm anyway from the point at (7) above, but in the absence of buses you'll need to return to that point and proceed on past the Old Moat Garden Centre, over one roundabout and on to another. Turn left at the second roundabout onto the B280 and follow this road into Epsom, about a mile away; to reach Epsom station, turn left up the road immediately beyond the railway overbridge, soon arriving at the station which is on the left.

Disused railway exploration can bring many contrasting walking experiences: compare this tranquil and popular section of the Chichester-Midhurst walk (above) with the very urban end to the Kemp Town branch walk (below)!

A perfect day and a clear path - disused railway walking at its best along the course of the Chichester-Midhurst line.

Also published by S.B. Publications -
Walking the Disused Railways of Kent
by David Bathurst

This book is the definitive guide to exploring on foot the many
and diverse disused railways of Kent, from delightful country
branch lines past hop fields and bluebell woods to old colliery
lines and military railways, each with their own distinctive
character. Richly illustrated throughout, it is the indispensable
reference work for anyone wishing to explore this fascinating
aspect of Kent history and our transport heritage.

ISBN 978-1-85770-356-6